Doctors, Faith, and Courage

How a Healer, Faith, and Doctors Worked Together

The Lessons and Tools from Spirit on my Journey with Cancer.

BY

DEBRA MARTIN

"The pain you feel today is the strength you feel tomorrow."
-Stephen Richards

Contents

Author's Note

Throughout this book, I use the word "God", but this does not mean I am limiting it to only the word "God". You may call your God something else like Heavenly Father, Spirit, Guides, Source, Universe, The Divine, etc. When I say God in this book, I believe that God is the meaning of all, the One, but can come in many forms and have many different titles. Ultimately, God is Love.

I hope that after reading this book, you will become more aware of your inner connection and with what is available for each of us when we ask, connect, and listen. We are all deserving and we are all so very loved.

FOREWORD
By Susanne J. Wilson, MPA

If you or someone you love is living with a severe injury or illness, *Doctors, Faith, and Courage* will be a Godsend. Within these pages, you will find unexpected and exquisite gifts that arose when author Debra Martin, a renowned research medium and mystical healer, was diagnosed and treated for cancer.

When she was first diagnosed, Debra Martin's mind raced with questions. Is life ever going to be the same? Will people doubt the healing abilities of a healer who has cancer? What could an accomplished spiritual teacher and healer, one who experienced two near-death events and a serious illness years earlier, need to learn now from having cancer?

I must confess that, as a longtime fellow mediumship colleague and more recently, as a healing client of the author's, I was shocked that cancer would happen to one who is so firmly entrenched in helping people heal. And yet, that is exactly why cancer happened to the author, and why I encouraged her to share her story to help others.

Very early on in her treatment, Debra decided not only to accept but to rely upon the compassion of others. She blessed all the events during her treatment, both the good and the ugly, immediately in the moment. I highly recommend that you walk with Debra Martin on her path of discovering profound insights that make *Doctors, Faith, and Courage* a book sure to help thousands who seek the peace that surpasses all understanding.

Susanne J. Wilson, MPA, is an intuition and mediumship teacher and author of "Soul Smart: What the Dead Teach Us About Spirit Communication, 2nd edition".

1

MY VISION

In January of 2019, I came out of a deep sleep when I heard these words: "You need to finish your book as this will leave your legacy. Get this done now!"

At the time, I was finishing my book "Proof of Miracles", so these words didn't hold a lot of meaning for me. I already knew that this was true because my writings were about my life as a healer and medium. I didn't understand the urgency that I heard in those words.

I was in the editing process and working with my editor to have the book completed in about a month's time. The next step was deciding how I wanted to publish. I didn't forget those words, but I also didn't pay too much attention to them.

Not long after, however, they took an entire different meaning after I received some devastating news.

A month later in February, my daughter and I were Facetiming with my oldest daughter who lived in California. After saying goodbye so I could get to my 2:00 p.m. hair appointment on time, I pulled out of my subdivision turned on my radio. Though winter in Arizona wasn't very cold, I was still a little chilled that afternoon. I danced in my seat to the music despite the chill. Life was good.

When my cell phone rang, and I glanced down and saw it was a call from my doctor's office. I quickly turned off my music and answered.

"Good afternoon, Ms. Martin," came a polite voice from the other end. "I've tried to reach out several times today, so thank you for picking up."

My heart fell down into my stomach, and the joy I'd felt chatting with my girls and heading down the road quickly left me. *This can't be good*, I thought.

"Where are you right now?"

"Driving," I replied, one hand safely on the steering wheel.

"Are you able to go home?" the woman asked, and my nerves rose further.

"No," I said, "but I can pull over. One second."

I sat on the side of the road and turned up the heater in my car as I waited for whatever news was important enough for the doctor's assistant to call me multiple times.

"Your test came back," she explained. "You have cancer."

I went numb, trying to process words that I never thought I'd have to hear.

About a week prior, I had been experiencing a hemorrhoid that was bothering me for a few months. When it had started, I'd made an appointment to have it removed, but my doctor insisted it wasn't inflamed and should be left alone. Not long after, however, the hemorrhoid became very inflamed, painful, and annoying. It bothered me whenever I sat, went to the bathroom, and even my underwear irritated it.

When I was half awake one morning, I heard a stern voice say: "You need to get this hemorrhoid removed *now*." I immediately called the doctor that morning and scheduled the soonest appointment to get it removed.

My mind went back to 2015, when I'd had similar symptoms and gone to my doctor. Back then, I'd had a hemorrhoid removed and had pre-cancerous cells discovered. After surgery, everything came back clear, and it had been a miracle that I'd gone in when I did. This just reinforced my intuition now, and I knew better than to ignore this voice.

The doctor was surprised to see me in the office, as I was not due to see her again until later in the year. I remembered explaining that I had come in to have a hemorrhoid removed that had been bothering me. She told the nurse to get me ready, as she would need to take a look at the hemorrhoid first.

I bent over the table, laying on my stomach and feeling a bit uncomfortable. She checked and agreed that it was inflamed and could be removed if I chose to do so. She then walked up to the front of the table by my head and leaned over.

"Are you sure you want to remove this?" she asked me. "It's going to hurt and cause you more pain for about three weeks. You don't need to remove this."

I replied, "Yes, it's already painful. I would rather have three weeks of pain and then have it be gone."

"Are you sure?" the doctor questioned me again, this time in a stern voice.

I had nodded at her. "Intuitively, I know this needs to come out. Please remove it."

I had to remove my humanness in that moment and trust what I heard as it came from Spirit. When I received strong messages like that one, they outweighed any of my own thoughts and fears. I had a strong sense of knowing what I needed to do that even overrode what a doctor told me.

Even though just over a week had passed, I still easily remembered my doctor walking to the back of the exam table. She had asked the nurse to hand her the scalpel and scissors. In that moment I had thought, *Really? Do you have to say that so loud?* The entire situation that I'd insisted upon was now even more scary. She had numbed me first, which hurt the most.

Afterward, she asked me if I wanted to see the hemorrhoid, and was surprised when I said yes. It was the size of a kidney bean, but the color of a dried pinto-bean. It didn't have any red veins running through it like I thought it would. The doctor and I then discussed if we should even send it for biopsy, and even though she felt it looked normal, she decided to send it just to be safe.

Now, in the car, I listened to her say that the hemorrhoid came back cancerous. It was an understatement to say I was shocked. Everything in my world came to a complete stop. She continued to describe the type of cancer, but I wasn't able to comprehend any of it. Overwhelmed with shock, my heart beat rapidly and my chest felt like a stack of bricks was placed on it.

I knew right then that I was having a panic attack. I looked in my rear view mirror and saw that my face had gone dangerously pale. Lightheaded-ness attacked me, and I felt like I would pass out. With my right hand on the phone, I learned my head on the center console. My other hand reached for my necklace, grasping the cross and Mother Mary medal that hung from it. At that moment, I needed to feel like I wasn't alone.

"I'm so sorry, Debra," the doctor was repeating in my ear. "I honestly can't believe it myself. I would like you to come in tomorrow so we can discuss the next form of treatment with a specialist."

I felt my hand shaking on my phone, and realized that I couldn't drive to my hair appointment as I could hardly concentrate. My mind was somewhere else as I numbly agreed with my doctor and hung up. I turned my car around slowly, feeling my legs shaking uncontrollably. Thank God I was only around the corner from home.

When I walked back into the house, my daughters were still Facetiming one another. They asked what was wrong and why I was back home. I could not get any words out, but they could tell by the look in my eyes and by my body language that something was really wrong.

"Were you in a car accident?" they asked.

I shook my head.

"Well, what happened?" they questioned again, but I literally could not get the words out of my mouth.

I didn't know how to deliver the news without saying the "c" word. I sat on the couch and my youngest daughter, age seventeen, put her arm around me. "Mom, it's okay," she reassured me. "What's wrong?"

I then voiced the words I never wanted to say, and as soon as I saw my daughter's reactions, I promised myself I would only say them to a few people. I was not going to give this any more power that it already had.

Once the declaration was out, everything flowed in slow motion. I looked on the phone screen and watched my oldest daughter, age thirty, crumble. She put her hand over her mouth and said, "No, mom. No, this can't be right!" as tears ran from her eyes.

Then I heard my youngest daughter cry next to me, and I couldn't stop the tears, either. My heart ached with sadness when I saw how life-shattering my news was to my children. I felt the incredible love we had for each other despite the disbelief we all felt, and the unknown that lay ahead of us. I knew I needed to make calls to my sons later.

"Mom," Allison, my youngest daughter, began a few moments later, "I can drive you to your hair appointment, if you'd like. That should take your mind off of this, since we can't do anything yet."

When did she become so wise? I thought. She also knew how important I felt my hair appointments were. I never missed one unless

I was sick or there was an emergency. *I'm not sick,* I thought. *Or am I?* My life and my children's lives were all about to change from this one phone call.

Once the rest of my children found out, everyone took action. I felt like I had my team around me, even though we weren't all next to each other. My oldest son lived in Cleveland, Ohio with his wife and two children. He started looking into the Cleveland Clinic for information on treating anal cancer. My youngest son was working at Johns Hopkins Hospital, and he started talking to his friends who were oncologists. Knowing that both of my boys lived by two of the most credible treatment centers for cancer, and even anal cancer, made me feel like this may play out as well as I was hoping for.

Was it a coincidence that they both lived near two prestigious cancer treatment centers? That's when my mind began to wonder if they had both been guided by Spirit to move to these two areas in the last year because Spirit knew what was going to happen. Though I found some comfort in this idea, I was still worried about potentially having to leave my hometown for my treatments. After all, this meant that the cancer would have spread to other areas of my body, like my liver, stomach, or lungs. These treatments would be more intense, and would require me living with my children so they could take care of me.

I ultimately knew thoughts were energy and I needed to keep my energy moving in a positive direction.

All my children were so supportive and let me know that however bad the situation was, they had my back. We were going to kick cancer's ass! I could see the concern on their faces and heard it in their voices during many phone calls. Instead of letting the news overwhelm them so they could not function, they took that energy and put it into action. They stayed positive and started doing research so they would have all the facts on what needed to happen next once we found out more from my doctors.

Later that evening, my oldest son called and asked if I would like him to be at my side tomorrow when I went to the doctors. I told him I would be fine.

"I know you will be fine, mom," he replied, "but think about it. I am talking about being there for your emotional support. You don't know what you're going to feel after hearing this news. I can take the next flight out and be there for your appointment. I could be there to hug you during and after."

"No, sweetheart," I insisted, though my heart warmed when I heard the concern and love in his voice. "It'll be best if you wait. I may need more help in the upcoming weeks."

After hanging up, I took a moment to steady my breath and relax my mind, so I would be ready to face what was coming the next day.

2

MY MEETING WITH MY RECTAL DOCTOR

My neighbor, Patty drove me to my doctor appointment the following day. I was too fragile to go alone, and she became my first angel at my side.

As I sat in the waiting room, the nurse came in to greet me. She came right up to me and said, "Oh my goodness, Debra! I was the one who read the report. When I saw your name, I was so upset."

She started to cry, and we embraced. We had become close over the years, sharing about our kids and grandkids. It was easier going to these appointments knowing I was going to get to see Nurse Leslie. She walked me and Patty back into a room. Now, sitting in the same room I had sat in many times before, I felt unsettled for the first time. I was nervous to hear the details of her findings.

Pat must have seen the fear in my eyes because she reached over and held my hand. "Debra, you're going to be okay," she said tearfully. "I love you."

When the doctor came in, I immediately noticed the sadness in her eyes. I could tell when I met her gaze that there was also regret.

"I am so sorry," she said, taking a seat on the stool in the corner. "I hesitated to remove the hemorrhoid and send it for biopsy. Everything looked normal. I'm shocked it came back with cancer."

In my heart, I knew her words were sincere, but in my mind I wasn't sure how to feel. Should I be angry? If she hadn't listened to me about removing this, there would be cancer spreading throughout my entire body. And, if she'd removed it months earlier, maybe I wouldn't even have cancer now.

I decided not to worry about all the what-ifs and chose to stay present in the moment. There was nothing I could do to change how everything had transpired. "I'm shocked, too," I said aloud. This has been devastating news for all of us. Now we need to know more about this cancer so we can put a plan into action."

I immediately asked her if I could please put my two sons on a speaker so they could listen in and ask questions, and she said yes.

She explained that the cancer was from the HPV virus, and that it had turned into something called Squamous Cell Carcinoma. "This type of cancer forms in the cells that line the anus," she told us. "It's most common type of anal cancer, and most patients treated for it have an excellent prognosis."

"What type of treatment will I need?" I asked quickly.

"I'll set you up with an oncologist," she replied rather vaguely. "He'll be the one to come up with at treatment plan. But don't worry; you'll be in good hands."

This was better news than what my sons thought they were going to hear. They'd been researching and had seen many more terrifying options that what my doctor had just shared. We all felt that we needed to take this one step at a time and see what the oncologist thought tomorrow. Before they hung up, my sons thanked my doctor for her time.

We all felt that this wasn't going to be as bad as we had thought. A positive wave of energy fell over the room, and a bit of hope lit in my heart.

"You'll need to see the radiation oncologist tomorrow," my doctor said. "We can set an appointment for early in the morning."

I thanked her, knowing that she was aware that I had a flight the next afternoon to go help my daughter in California, who was having surgery.

As I left the room, Leslie hugged me again. The doctor approached and said, "Debra, this is not going to be that hard. You may have radiation once a week. Everything is going to be okay."

The next day as I headed to the radiation oncologists' office, I thought, *this is not how I wanted to spend my Valentine's Day*. I always said that coincidences and/or synchronicities seemed to happen on significant dates so that they were easier for us to remember. I knew there had to be a reason for this, I just didn't know it yet.

My best friend, Amy drove me to this appointment. I called her one of my angels, she gave me strength and let me know I wasn't going to do this alone. She was at my side each step of the way.

I took a deep breath as we pulled into the parking lot, and when I spotted the sign "Cancer Center", everything became real. I still couldn't believe this was happening. A heaviness grew in my chest as the unknown of what we were about to face settled on me. I did everything I could to stop tears from flowing.

Amy and I entered the building and went into the waiting room. It was full of chairs and many tables that offered coffee, tea, treats, magazines, and puzzles to engage patients. At the sign-in counter, the nurse behind a pane of glass greeted me with a gentle smile.

"You must be Debra Martin," she said in an endearing voice.

I relaxed a little; her words felt like a hug as she handed me a clipboard and asked me to fill out some paperwork. When I was finished, my name was called and Amy and I walked back to another, larger room.

A nurse's station was the center of this room, its walls made of many doors. I slowly took in everything, including one of the open doors that looked like it lead into a doctor's office. As we walked past the nurse's station, several people bustled past us while others stood by high counters covered in computer screens. The nurse leading us led us to the left now, toward the exam room meant for me, and everything seemed to break down into slow motion.

This is where it all begins, I thought nervously. The heaviness came back to my chest and my mind became foggy as Amy and I took our seat in this little room with three chairs, a counter, and an exam table. Sensing my worry, Amy reached over and placed her hand on my knee.

"Are you okay?" she asked.

Unable to hold it back, I shook my head no and finally let the tears fall. There were too many consuming emotions to handle. "Thank you for being here with me," I whispered to Amy. "I couldn't do this without you."

The radiation oncologist came in a few minutes later. I reminded myself that this was the doctor who would set the radiation treatments I might need based on the type of cancer I had. He immediately had a smile on his face, as if he was pleased to see me. When he reached out his hand to introduce himself, I learned that he had the same first name as my son.

"Would you mind," I asked, "if I called my daughter-in-law so she can listen and ask questions? I'd like to record this, too, if that's alright."

He nodded. "Of course, Debra," he replied. "In fact, let's put your phone near me so that recording picks up my voice clearly."

I thanked him, so grateful for the compassion in his voice.

"My rectal doctor told me this was going to be an easy conversation," I said, "but I'm still nervous."

"Well," the doctor replied, taking a seat. "You do have anal cancer, Debra. As you know, it came from the HPV virus, and you will require a series of intense radiation and chemotherapy to beat this."

I glanced at Amy, and saw that her face had gone very pale. "But," I began slowly, "I was told this would be easily treated. What you're saying sounds like the complete opposite."

He gave me a serious look, as if to confirm this terrifying news. "I know the words are frightening, but you are not alone in this. Tell me," he added, changing the subject a little to try and comfort me, "what do you do for a living?"

I shifted uncomfortably in my chair, not sure how to answer this. It was easy to cover up and say, "I'm an author." Instead, I gathered my courage and went with the truth: "This is going to sound strange, but I am a healer. I've healed others who've struggled with cancer. It's not easy for me to say this, because I'm having a hard time accepting that I now have cancer. Healers have a hard time healing themselves."

What would my clients think if they knew I had cancer and was seeing a doctor?

"Debra," my doctor began, and I braced myself for his response. "You are the vessel. The healing comes through you."

I looked at him, surprised by his response. I swore that Spirit took over and was talking through my doctor in that moment.

"It's not your body doing the healing," he continued. "Your body is going to take on things in life that you don't have control over."

Wow. It was so powerful for me to hear these words out of my doctor's mouth. I knew then that this was the doctor chosen by Spirit to help me on this journey. I was in the right hands and God showed me this through this man's words.

"I do have a lump," I shared with him, "in my left side groin area that feels like a large ball. My rectal doctor knows about this, and I have an appointment with my OBGYN next week."

My doctor glanced at my chart, then said, "I'd like to do a quick scan while you're here, Debra. Then we can re-group in this room."

He left the room to get a nurse who would lead me alone to an-other area behind the nurse's station. This place was bigger, sterile, and very cold. She asked me to take off my capris and stood me in front of a machine very similar to the PET scan. After positioning me on a table, she placed stickers on each of my hips and one in the cen-ter of my lower abdomen as markers to guide the machine.

She told me to relax as she left the room to begin the scan, and I took a deep breath and closed my eyes. Afterward, I got dressed and went back to the exam room where Amy was waiting. It didn't take long for the doctor to return.

A serious expression was back on his face, and I knew that he had bad news right away. "Debra," he began, "that lump is exactly what I thought. The cancer has spread to two of your lymph nodes. The tumor on the inside of your anal wall is also cancerous. You'll need to get a PET scan as soon as possible so we can make sure this hasn't spread to other areas of your body."

I swallowed, trying to take all of this in. "What happens next?" I asked.

"Once we have the results of that scan, I'll consult with my team and come up with a plan. You'll see a radiation therapist daily, and you'll have prescriptions to take as well."

This was so much to process I asked him to repeat everything again, then I couldn't help but ask another question: "How painful will this be?" I couldn't imagine getting radiation in such a sensitive area of my body. How would it affect my ability to go to the bath-room? Fear started to set in and anxiety crept through me.

"Debra," my doctor answered calmly, "you won't feel pain right away. It will occur later, from the cumulative radiation treatments. You will feel fatigue, swelling, and soreness as well, but let's not worry about this yet. Every person is different, and you are in very good health and physical shape. You'll lose a lot of weight and muscle tone in this process, so keep working out and avoid all carbs and sugar."

"I can do that," I agreed. It was a lot to take in, and I was so glad my daughter-in-law was listening and Amy was taking notes so I could be present with my feelings.

"Depending on the scan results, we'll have two plans to consider going forward," my doctor said. "Plan 1, which involves thirty days of radiation, will happen if this cancer hasn't spread to any other areas. Plan 2, which involves you finding another clinic and treatment center specifically for anal cancer, will happen if the cancer has spread."

I mentioned my two sons, who both lived by clinics and hospitals that could help me if Plan 2 took place. "That's great," my doctor said. "You'll need a much help as you can with this type of treatment. Plan 1, however, is what I would consider curable, Debra. And, even after treatments take place, sometimes cancer cells can still show up on a follow-up PET scan, so please be prepared for that."

I smiled at him. "I'll be different," I said with confidence. "As a healer, I'll be doing my part in the healing process."

Well, that was a strong statement, I thought, surprising myself a little.

"If anyone can make this happen, she will," Amy spoke up encouragingly.

Her words helped remind me that I knew God was on my side. I didn't come back from a near-death experience to have my life end like this. Still, my humanness did come out to my play and made new questions surface in my mind: *Is this all part of my mission on earth?*

I don't feel like I have control over my body, but I do have control over how I'm going to face this. As a healer, speaking about this is going to make me very vulnerable. I've got to let these unsettling thoughts and emotions go.

I knew that I had to let go and give my trust to God. I had to remove my humanness and listen to my higher self, my soul. I was not alone.

After my doctor shared these two plans with me, he mentioned that I needed to go to another center to meet with Dr. Stephanie.

"But Debra has a flight in a couple hours," Amy said. "Her daughter is coming out of surgery later today and she's supposed to be there to see her."

In a very calm but stern voice, my doctor said, "You shared with me that your daughter's surgery is an elective surgery, but I think you need to miss that flight and meet with Dr. Stephanie instead. Yours is a matter of life and death, and we need to start this plan as soon as we can."

"I think it's important for me to be around family right now," I said. "That emotional support is really what I need now."

He looked at me for a moment before saying, "I understand. You should still keep your appointment with Dr. Stephanie. However, your PET scan can take a few more days while you go see your family."

As I left, I was overwhelmed. I thought back to the night my son offered to come sit with me to hold my hand when I heard this news. *Wow!* I thought. Now I understand what he was saying. *If I had any idea how bad things actually were, I would have taken him up on his offer.* I may have had him carry me to the car. I could hardly walk, speak, or think.

When we reached the parking lot, Amy said, "What's going on? We should be hiking!" Once we got in the car, she asked if I was angry with my doctor.

It took me a moment to consider her question. I didn't really know how I was feeling; should I be angry? I had so much else on my mind that I couldn't begin to conquer any of the "what-ifs?".

As we drove to the chemotherapy doctor, I called my youngest son and told him that I recorded the entire meeting with the oncologist. My voice shook a little when I informed him that this was much worse than we were initially told. Despite the strength in his tone, I could tell that he was very worried for me..

As I settled into yet again another doctor's office, I was greeted by Dr. Stephanie. Her voice was calm and her smile was gentle. I could feel her compassion when she shook my hand. From the kindness in her voice, I could tell that to her I wouldn't just be a patient; I would "matter."

When she introduced herself, I was shocked to find out her first name was the same as my older daughter's. I couldn't help but stop and appreciate this turn of fate for a moment. Both of my doctors' first names were the first names of my two oldest children. Spirit was once again letting me know they had my back, and I was being guided to the right doctors.

Dr. Stephanie was very kind, sensitive, and beautiful. Spirit knew that I needed a doctor who would give me as much of her time as I needed. I started the recording on my phone, and called my daughter-in-law so she could listen to our appointment and take notes.

"Debra," she began, and her voice was soft and reassuring. "We're going to wait for the results of PET scan before knowing how to definitively move forward. For now, we are going to place a port in your upper chest that will be used for infusions, blood work, and hydration procedures over the next six weeks."

I looked at her for a moment, feeling inundated. "What will that be like?" I asked.

Dr. Stephanie smiled. "It'll hardly be noticeable, don't worry," she assured me.

Just then, the reality of my situation pressed in heavily on my shoulders. Unable to stop myself, I started to cry. The thought of having a port put under my skin made everything very real. "Is that really necessary?" I asked, clearing my throat.

"Yes," Dr. Stephanie said, handing me a tissue. "It's extremely important, as the infusions can only be given to you in this manner."

She went on to explain that the medicine for the infusion was called Mitomycin, a type of vesicant. A vesicant was a chemical that caused extensive tissue damage and blistering if it escaped the veins. The amount that I received would depend on many factors, including my height and weight, my general health, and the type of cancer that was being treated.

"You'll likely end up needing a port like this no matter what," Dr. Stephanie added. "It's easier to take blood out of instead of having your veins poked all the time."

I beg to differ, I thought, but tried to give her an understanding nod.

As if this information wasn't enough, I now had to be prepared to hear what the plans for moving forward could be. I settled into my seat and took a deep breath so I could fully concentrate on Dr. Stephanie's words. The recording was already going on my phone, but I double-checked it anyway, making sure I would have all the important information to share with my children later.

"Dr. Stephanie," I began when she was done speaking. "Dr. Steven told me earlier that this plan would lead to me being 100% cured. But I'd like to hear what your honest thoughts are."

This was a big question, and I felt my heart pounding as she carefully considered her answer. "I agree," she said after a few moments. "This is absolutely curable."

As our appointment came to an end, I hung up with my daughter-in-law. Before doing so, I learned that the entire time she was at her own child's doctor appointment the entire time. She impressed me further by texting her notes in a group for the rest of the family to see the upcoming plans. This took so much emotional stress and work off my shoulders.

Dr. Stephanie ordered my blood work and stated that I needed to get blood drawn downstairs before I left. I glanced at my watch and noticed that time was running short in order for me to be able to catch my flight at the airport. Things kept getting in my way.

I looked over at Amy, worried. "Is Spirit trying to tell me I need to stay home?" I asked her. "I don't know if I'll make this flight!"

Luckily, the blood work went fast I was out of the cancer center and soon on my way home. Thank God I packed my suitcase the previous night and it was ready to go. I called my driver, JT, for the third time to see if he could get me to the airport by 5:45 p.m. for my 7:00 p.m. flight. I had canceled and rescheduled my flight three times that day. Southwest Airlines was so kind and accommodating to me due to my situation. I was cutting it close.

I raced home, took my pup, Layla out as she would be flying with me, and grabbed a quick bite to eat as I had nothing to eat all day. By the time I was finished, JT was waiting outside. At the airport I checked my bags at the curb, went through the TSA approved lane, and was at my gate with some time to spare.

3

WALKING STICKS, DANDELIONS, AND WISHES

As I walked through the airport, I felt numb. I was viewing everything and everyone around me as if I was frozen in time. I saw a couple with two young children getting ready to go on vacation. I thought to myself, *will I ever be able to go on vacation with my grandkids? Will I ever go on a vacation again? Will I ever be able to walk through life again without the worry that nothing would ever happen to me? Will I ever laugh again?*

I sat down in a near-empty row near my gate, wrestling with these new emotions I'd never experienced before. Life had just taken a completely unexpected turn, and I had no idea what was coming. I kept watching people as they bustled toward their flights or hurried in the opposite direction toward baggage claim and undoubtedly loved ones waiting for them. I wished I could tell each of them that they didn't know how good they had it. Health was everything. Without good health, one had many limitations. I was about to learn how limiting my life would become.

As I found my seat on the plane, it took so much to hold back the tears. After all, I was supposed to be flying to my daughter's house to take care of her and have a fun-filled weekend with my grandson. Now, I no longer knew what that looked like. I felt like I was under a heavy blanket and couldn't breathe. I was not going to be able to come up for air until I knew the results of that PET scan.

Maybe I should have stayed home and done this tomorrow, I thought. *This waiting is going to be torturous.*

When I landed in California, I grabbed Layla and went to the baggage claim. While I was waiting for my bags, I decided to reach out to a dear friend of mine and share my news. I thought it would be a good idea to do this now, before I reached my daughter's house, since I probably wouldn't have the time later.

As the phone rang, my heart beat faster. "Hi," I said when he picked up. "This is Debra."

A familiar laugh sounded from the other end of the phone. "I know it's you," he said. "What's up? Where are you? There's lots of noise in the background."

"I'm at the airport in California," I replied. "I'm here to take care of my daughter who just had some elective surgery."

"Oh no! I hope she's doing okay."

"That isn't why I'm calling," I said. "But yes, she'll be fine. I have some terrible news to share with you. Remember how we promised that if anything bad happened we would let each other know?"

His voice was full of concern when he replied, "Why? What's going on, Deb?"

"I have cancer," I said, hardly able to get the words out.

There was silence for a moment, and I could tell he was also shedding tears. Then the questions came: "When did you find this out? Where is it and how bad?"

After explaining everything, he immediately asked if he could come out and take care of me. I let him know that my family and friends at home were going to help me, so there was no need. After that, I felt the tone of the conversation shift. "Well," he said, his voice more guarded now. "I hope everything goes well for you, Deb. Take care."

And just like that, our conversation ended. I was shocked with his sudden lack of compassion, and how he'd just shut the door on me. Since I didn't need his help, he didn't want any more communication with me. I never thought this would be his response, as he was always a kind and loving person in my life. We had been friends for over thirty years.

Really? I thought. *Did that just happen?*

After getting my bags, I decided I needed to sit on one of the benches inside the terminal so I could process what happened. I really had expected a more loving, embracing response over the phone. I realized that some people handled hard news in different ways: some people would stick with me through the healing process while others would not at all.

He made this all about himself, I thought. *He wasn't able to come out and help me, so he didn't want anything to do with me. Maybe this is too much for him to handle. But why would he be thinking of himself when I am the one in need of support? Having his help over the phone would have helped me greatly.*

I sighed and took out my phone to call an Uber. I had to trust that I was experiencing this for a reason. God was showing me who had my back and who didn't. Even though I didn't understand all the why's, I was okay with his decision, and I was grateful for each person that was able to give or not give support to me.

After my experience with this phone call, I asked my family and a couple close friends to not share this with anyone. A few of them felt that the more people I shared this with, the more prayers I would have out there for me. I didn't feel the same way. I felt that I wanted to be very choosy with who I would share this with, as it was very private and sacred. I felt that if I wasn't choosy, people would start telling other people and the gossip would begin. Words are very powerful. I didn't want people saying, "I feel so sorry for Debra. Debra has cancer. Can you believe Debra who is a healer has cancer?" Who knows what else would be said from there?

I made my way outside to wait for my Uber, and noticed it was already dark and the weather was cold. I reached for my jacket and put it on as my ride arrived. I didn't feel like chatting, but the driver was very talkative. I let her tell me about her struggles and what was going on in her life. I was half-listening, and responded very little.

"Oh, what street should I turn down?" she asked me a while later.

My mind was in a fog, and even though I'd taken this drive many times, I wasn't sure what to say. *Shouldn't she know where she's going with her map?* The girl took a wrong turn, and we ended up behind my daughter's street in an alley. *How did she get us here?*

Once she'd gotten us back on the main road, my driver pulled up to a house. I peered out the window, not recognizing where we'd arrived. *Am I really losing it,* I thought, *or do I not know my own daughter's house?*

"This isn't the address to the house I gave you," I said to my driver.

She glanced at her phone, then said, "yeah. It's just up the street. Would you like me to drive up to it?"

I stared at her. *Really? Does she think I want to drag my luggage and my dog out of her car and up the road a full block?* I shook my head. "Could you please drive right up to the house? I'd like to get all my belongings out there."

Twenty seconds later, we were at the right house, and I couldn't wait to get out of the car. It seemed like I was in a bad dream. I stepped outside and placed Layla on the sidewalk, then went back to the trunk. The girl gave me no assistance, waiting in her car until I'd closed her trunk. She said goodbye, and I decided to wish her the best with what she had going on in her life. Obviously her head was in a fog, too.

It was starting to drizzle, so I hurriedly took Layla out of her carrier so she could go potty before we went inside. When I looked up at the house, I saw everyone was hanging out in the living room.

As I walked into my daughter's house I became very emotional. I saw her lying on the couch and my grandson ran right up to me. Receiving his hug was just what I needed. As I held onto him, I realized that I would to do anything for my kids or grandkids, and that included surviving this beast inside of me. They were the angels God gifted to me, and I was beyond blessed to have them in my life.

Later that night in bed, I thought more about Amy's question: *Are you angry with your doctor?* I wondered if she had taken my hemorrhoid out last November, would I be going through all of this now? Maybe the cancer would not have spread, because at that time I didn't feel the lump in my left groin area. What if she hadn't sent the hemorrhoid out for biopsy? Where would I be now? Would the cancer continue to spread? Would I even have known I had cancer? Would my OBGYN have sent me for a scan or biopsied the lump? Those were longer processes that could give the cancer more time to grow.

Thinking of all of those questions was not serving me. It caused me more unnecessary worry that I could not change. All I could do now was pray for a good outcome. I finished my prayer, turned on my side, and cried myself to sleep.

I found myself waking and crying throughout the night, and was unable to stop more tears during the next day. Not having an answer for what I was about to face weighed heavily on my mind. Everything around me became emotional. I was grateful to be able to sit next to my daughter, take Layla out for a walk, and for having time with my grandson. I tried to make each moment special as I was not sure if I would ever have any moments like this again.

Liam and Layla enjoyed our walks, and they were the highlight of my day, too. As we made our way down the sidewalk in his neighborhood, we spotted a large stick was in our way.

"Look!" I exclaimed. "Look at this cool stick!"

I handed it to him, and the awed expression on his face made it seem like he had never seen a stick before. Wonder filled his eyes as he grasped what he clearly thought was the coolest toy he has ever received. I taught him how to sweep the ground with the stick, touch the low tree branches, and even stick the stick in the mud.

As soon as the end of the stick was covered in mud, he let out a big laugh. Then he looked at his hands and stared at the grime coating his palms and fingers. "Oh no!" he gasped.

"It's okay," I assured him, and held up my own hands in demonstration. "Just take your hands like this and brush them on your pants. Now it's all gone!"

Liam stared at me with unsure eyes. The idea of wiping his hands on his clothes was crazy to him. I was sure his parents told him not to do this, but Grandma Dee Dee was saying it was okay and it was fun.

When we got back, we had to place Liam's stick by the front door so that he knew exactly where to find it for our next walk. Later that day when we went out, his hands got dirty again. This time, Liam looked up at me with a huge grin on his face and just wiped his hands on his pants. He was so proud of what he was doing, but I could tell he felt he might be doing wrong. I wondered if he would do this with his parents or just me.

I think that as grandparents we earned the right to break the rules once in a while.

The next day we took a longer walk. It was a beautiful, overcast day, and the perfect weather to wear a jacket outside. Back in Arizona, I wouldn't have been able to take a stroll in the extreme heat. The neighborhood was full of cute houses, all in different colors and sizes.

Between the driveways and the grass patches that ran along the curbs were sidewalks that went for miles.

This was always one of my favorite places to walk. It was only a few miles from the beach, and I enjoyed breathing in the air and feeling the freshness of the ocean against my face. A familiar sense of peace washed over me.

As we went, I saw a dandelion in the grass and quickly said, "Oh my goodness! Look at what I found!"

Liam curiously watched me pick the flower. I showed him how to hold it and make a wish.

"After your wish," I explained, "we blow the puffs into the air!" The white seeds billowed into the wind, caught in the light breeze and illuminated by the bright sunshine. I glanced down at my grandson's grin and took a deep breath, appreciating the special moment between us. I had wished that I would be healthy and whole, so I could live a long life to continue to be around my family. He giggled so hard as the dandelion seeds drifted away. "More! More!" he exclaimed happily.

We continued to search for dandelions that day, and each day after. It became our quest. He learned fast; when he picked the dandelion, he said, "No yellow, Dee Dee." He now knew not to pick the yellow flowers, only the ones that had the fuzzy white puffs. Then he held the dandelions aloft like they were his prizes.

We always blew and made a wish together each and every time. In fact, when I left, my daughter said he became obsessed with taking walks with his stick and finding dandelions. Whenever he found one, he threw a fit if they didn't stop for him to pick it and make a wish. Hearing this brought me much happiness, knowing I left an imprint for him to remember me by.

As I was helping my daughter recover from surgery, she also helped me. I didn't know who helped who more. She set me up with my own Google Calendar and input all my upcoming doctor appointments.

When she shared the calendar the entire family, it connected everyone so they could be part of my care plan.

One afternoon two days after my arrival, Stephanie was feeling better. She said we needed to go to Best Buy, as she had something she needed to pick up. When the two of us walked to the counter, she asked the associate to get something that was on hold.

When he returned, he said, "I need a driver's license from Debra Martin."

I gave the young man a confused look. Why would he need my ID? But I gave it to him with no questions asked.

He left for a moment, then returned with a new rose gold computer that had my oldest son's name on it. Now I was really confused.

I glanced at my daughter and asked, "Did you just purchase this for your daughter?"

She shook her head with a smile. "No, Mom. This is for you."

"What?" I still didn't understand.

"Mom," Stephanie continued, "us kids all chipped in to buy you a new computer so you can be mobile with your work. We know you have been having issues with your computer at home, and we wanted to make things easier for you. You have enough going on that you don't need to worry about this, too."

Tears began to fill my vision as I listened to her kind words. The fact that all my children searched, discussed, and decided to do this for me without me asking was beyond amazing. I was speechless and tears of joy rolled down my cheeks. We hugged, then we called the boys one at a time and told the story of how oblivious I was. They all had a good laugh on my account.

My daughter set everything up on the computer, and even bought me wireless headphones for my healing sessions. We also researched and found an app that would record from my iPhone as an mp3 file to send to my clients. I didn't know this existed. The sound quality from the headphones was so much clearer compared to the headphones I was using on my old computer.

My children told me that no matter what happened, I was going to be fine. Thanks to them, I could now do my work from anywhere. This was the greatest gift I could have ever received. I felt so blessed and grateful for what they just did. They had begun taking care of me in ways I would have never thought they would. This took so much pressure off of me.

They were also concerned about my health insurance, as well as my regular bills as soon as hospital expenses started coming my way. They knew that with me being the owner of my company I had no paid PR or vacation time.

I assured my children that I had very good health insurance and that I had enough money in my savings to cover my expenses during the time I would need to take off of work. Depending on how bad the cancer was and how extensive the treatments needed to be, things may not turn out the way I expected.

It was possible that I'd have to live with either one of my sons if I needed to receive treatment at one of the top medical clinics. My insurance would not cover those bills that would take place outside of my network, and I could potentially be responsible for many thousands of dollars. We were also well aware that if I could not pay these high bills, the clinic would go after any and all of my assets. They would do anything to collect their money and could even take my house away from me.

I was already stressed as to what level of cancer I had, and now my sons were making me worry about more unknown factors. After coming to this realization, I let them know I had to stay positive, take one thing at a time, and talk about each challenge as it came. I trusted God and I knew that He would take care of me either way.

My boys didn't appreciate this response, saying I needed to be realistic and plan ahead for what may come. However, they honored my wishes and put the discussion to rest for now. We all knew that the following week we would know more from the PET scan.

That long weekend with my daughter was the beginning of my healing process. She was the first one who took care of me when I was very fragile. She hugged me when I cried. She listened to me voice all my fears of the unknown. She held my hand so that I would not be alone until I had my PET scan.

If I had stayed home alone, I would have spent a long weekend of crying alone as my mind did more wondering than it needed to. Stephanie was my rock and kept me focused on the positive. She embraced me with her love during this very crucial time.

By the time I left, Stephanie was up and around like she hadn't just had surgery. We both played our roles for one another, and even though the timing of me going out to California seemed bad at first, it turned out to be divine timing.

Family has a way of making everything bad go away, even if it is for a few minutes. Being there allowed me to breathe life without feeling the heavy weight that was on my chest. I was able to focus on them and not on me. I was very grateful for the time I was able to spend with my oldest daughter. It was a gift.

Now I needed to prepare myself for what was to come: finding the answers to the unknown.

The next day, I was prepared for the PET scan at Sonoran Lab Imaging, which was just fifteen minutes from my home. I didn't have anything to eat or drink six hours prior to the scan and I had limited my physical activity for the last twenty-four hours. I was told to hydrate myself very well, eat a high protein diet, and to not consume carbs or sugars the day prior. Carrots, peas, and corn were off limits, too, as they were high in sugar.

When Amy picked me up early in the morning, I could tell she saw the tiredness in my eyes. I didn't get much sleep the night before. My mind would not stop racing, and I spent many hours crying and in prayer.

Amy was very kind, however, and let me think quietly as we drove. I could not stop the nervous flow of questions barreling through my head: What was the scan going to reveal? Where was this cancer in my body? Would it be limited to the anal wall and lower lymph nodes, or had it traveled to other areas of my body? I was trying to stay positive, but my humanness was coming out to play. I knew that the next two hours at the imaging lab were going to be hard.

"Debra?" one of the technicians called, and I stood from my seat in the waiting room after squeezing Amy's hand one more time. She wasn't able to go back with me, due to the fact that the PET scan dye contained radioactive tracers.

The technician led me down a hallway, leaving the noise of the waiting room behind us. After entering another small room, he asked if I had any zippers on my clothing.

"Just the one on my pants," I replied.

"You'll need to change into this gown, then," the technician said, and handed me a blue colored gown with a polite smile. "And be sure to remove all of your jewelry. You'll be here for about an hour after we administer the dye."

I nodded, doing my best to look confident. After I had changed, I sat in a recliner in the center of the room. This chair took up most of the space, making it hard to walk anywhere else. I had a feeling that, if the foot recliner was up, no one would be able to walk through.

The technician came back in with a metal box. Inside was a metal tube that held the radioactive dye. It was in the metal container to protect the technician. I held my arm out, taking deep breaths so I would not shake.

The dye did not hurt going in; in fact, I didn't feel a thing. The technician let me know I needed to sit still, and couldn't even use my phone. He placed a white blanket on me and said he would check on me in thirty minutes.

I shut my eyes as he closed the door behind him and decided that I would take the time to meditate and pray. I envisioned that the white blanket represented God holding me in his white light and love. Immediately, a calm sense surrounded me. I was no longer concerned about being in this empty, cold room for an hour; I was in a peaceful space. During my prayers, I visualized the cancer being in a controlled space, and that it did not spread anywhere else in the body. I was going to stay positive and hold these thoughts during the entire PET scan process.

When it was time, the technician took me to conduct the PET scan. He positioned me on the exam table, where I had to keep both of my arms above my head the entire time. The technician placed a pillow under my head, which helped comfort both of my arms.

The exam table was connected to a scanner with a round, doughnut shaped hole in the middle. I listened as the technician explained to me that the table would slide into the machine as it rotated around me, taking a series of images.

"As these images are being taken," he said, "you'll hear a series of loud knocking sounds. Debra, it's very important that you remain still during the entire exam. You'll be the only one in the room."

"Okay," I replied. "How long is the scan?"

"About thirty to forty-five minutes," he said, and before he left he placed another white blanket over me. After turning off the lights, he said, "now it's time for you to relax."

Once again, I used the blanket to symbolize God's light and love holding me. I stayed in prayer and closed my eyes during most of the exam. In my prayers, I thanked God for this machine. It was going to reveal that my cancer was only in the controlled area that I had been envisioning in the last room.

As I was thanking God with my eyes closed, I saw a beautiful bright light come into the room. I quickly opened my eyes, thinking the technician turned the lights back on. To my surprise, everything was still dark. When I closed my eyes again, I saw and felt a light around me. I felt God's embrace and comfort. I had to now trust that God had a plan for me. Whatever that plan would be, I would walk through it knowing He would be by my side each and every step of the way.

When I left the PET exam, I felt at peace. I was no longer frightened. All was well and would be well, according to God's Plan. I was trusting the process.

I made my way back into the waiting room, and saw Amy sitting in the chair. Fear was clear on her face.

"How did it go?" she asked as soon as I reached her. She was trying so hard to comfort me during this difficult time, even though it was hard on her to watch me go through this.

Because Amy and I were very close and very much in sync with one another, I knew she could feel the shift of my energy from when I went back into the exam room and when I came out. We often felt each other's emotions even when we were not in the same room. We called one another revealing what we were feeling, wondering if the other person was feeling this way. Most of the times we were. She wanted to know every detail of what transformed me, and I told her as soon as we got in the car

Even though we were at peace, Amy and I were both very exhausted. Our emotions were all over the place, so as soon as she arrived back at my home, we hugged one another and told each other to get some well-deserved rest.

4

THE POWER OF WORDS:
CURABLE CANCER

The morning I was supposed to go into the hospital for my port to be installed, Amy arrived at 10:30. My procedure wasn't until 1:00, but we needed to arrive two hours prior so they could run lab work and prep me for surgery.

Even though the port installation was an outpatient procedure and I didn't have to stay overnight, I was still very nervous. I had a difficult time sleeping the night before, and for the last few days I often cried when I even thought about having this done. It was extremely traumatic knowing that having a port put in my body made the cancer undoubtedly real.

My doctor told me that the port device would be implanted under the skin of my chest below my collarbone. It was made of plastic, stainless steel, or titanium, and was about the size of a quarter, but thicker. I was told it will look like a small bump under my skin that would be hard for others to notice.

A few feet from the hospital entrance was the check-in desk, and after speaking with the woman there, I had to sit in the waiting area.

When my name was called, I signed all the proper paperwork for the procedure, got my hospital wristband, and paid my deductible. Next was heading to the lab where they drew my blood to check my platelet levels and made sure I was ready for surgery. This was quick and easy, and I knew it would be the last time I would get blood drawn from my arm.

A nurse led Amy and I to the elevator that took us up to the second floor, where both Amy and I had to sign in. They wanted Amy's phone number and had her write down what she was wearing in case they needed to identify her while I was in surgery. Amy was asked to stay in the waiting room, which was full of tables with coffee, tea, treats, and several televisions. I handed her my purse but kept my phone.

"I'll text you so you know what's going on," I told her before leaving.

The nurse took me through a set of double doors that she entered a code to open. We were the only ones walking down the halls, which were very quiet and filled with bright lights. Walking into the surgery prep room reminded me of an ER. All of the rooms were divided by tan curtains, and mine was the first on the left.

A large counter ran across the entire center, and behind it there were many nurses getting things ready for their patients. I watched as doctors wearing surgical gowns came up to the counter and quietly asked the nurses questions. There was a lot going on at once.

The lighting in my room was dimmer than the hallway, and gave the space a calmer feeling. The nurse here introduced herself and said she would be with me before and after surgery. "You can get changed into this gown," she said, handing me a blue material. "You can keep your leggings on, but remove everything from the waist up." She handed me a bag for my clothes and my shoes, and gave me a pair of socks to keep my feet warm.

Once I was changed, I lay on the bed with wheels, preparing myself for what came next. When my nurse returned, she asked me a series of questions to fill in on my chart, including my name, date of birth, and why I was here. Another nurse came in, and they began discussing with me why I was having this port installed. "You're getting this port placed because you have cancer," one of them said. The bluntness of her words blasted into my head, like the volume of a stereo being turned up to the max.

"Look," I began, unable to stop myself from telling her how I felt. "I understand what you're saying, but I don't even want to own the word 'cancer.' It's good to hear you say it, so I can try to own it. I just need to think of it as a temporary thing in my life that will go away."

The two nurses looked at each other for a moment, then I continued, "I know that I'm going to get through this and kill this disease. So, could you please say, 'you have *curable* cancer'? It's much easier for me to hear and digest."

I thought the nurse may take offense, but in fact she smiled at me and nodded. "I like this word," she replied. She seemed so pleased with my word choice that I felt she may even use this phrase in the future to help other patients.

The second nurse who was taking my vitals calmly asked me if I wanted a warm white blanket.

"Yes, please!" I replied with excitement. As she placed the white blanket on me, I asked, "would you like to know why I am so excited for this?"

She smiled at me and said, "I am sure it's because it's warm, and the room is quite cold."

I shook my head and said, "The white blanket represents God's white light and love. I can feel God's warmth hold me, letting me know He is with me and at my side through this entire procedure."

Both of the nurses at the same time said, "Wow, I love that!" They mentioned that they would say this to others when they offer them blankets to let them know they are never alone.

It was almost time for the surgery. A male nurse came in to tell me what was going to happen. "You have two choices, Ms. Martin," he explained. "You can get totally put under with anesthesia, or I can be given a small amount of medicine that will relax you during the procedure."

"I've gone through several surgeries in my lifetime already," I shared with him. "But I have to tell you that none of them have frightened me the way this one does."

"Well, this is a very simple procedure," he replied kindly. "It'll only take about fifteen minutes. I recommend getting the lighter sedation, because you won't remember what happens. However, if you request that we put you under, you'll have to be placed in a recovery room for an hour and a half before you can go home."

As nervous as I was about the surgery, I went with his first choice of being lightly sedated. I texted Amy that it was time: I was going into surgery. The nurse then took my phone and placed it in the bag with my other belongings.

As I was being wheeled into the surgery room, my heart began racing and I started second guessing my choice. Several nurses helped me move my body from one table to the next. They started prepping the room for the doctor, and I heard one of them mention that the doctor was running behind on his surgery.

Another nurse draped the right side of my chest with a blue cloth. She asked me to turn my head to the left and close my eyes. This was very unsettling, and I found it hard to keep my eyes closed. At one point I peeked and noticed them put a half ring over my chest and place another drape on it. It made me think of what was used in the operating rooms for women having a c-section to hide anything going on below their shoulders.

I could still see through the left side of the table, and a nurse came over to see how I was doing.

"Not very well," I replied, and glanced at the drape above me. "Can you please get this blue paper off of the right side of my face? And would you be able to make the opening bigger so I can get some air?"

He nodded and crumbled the blue paper to make the hole much bigger so I didn't feel so confined. "Debra," he began slowly, "you need to relax. Your heart rate is rising. If you don't calm down, the medicine that I am going to use to relax you when the doctor comes won't work."

The thought of the medicine not working made me even more nervous. I knew I had to stop concentrating on what was happening around me and take a few deep breaths. When I did, I imagined God holding me. In my mind, I heard *You got this! Everything is going to be okay.*

"Are you claustrophobic?" the nurse asked.

"I never thought of myself as being claustrophobic," I replied.

"Well, do you like to wear turtlenecks, or do they bother you?"

I thought for a moment, then said, "I am not a fan of them." I think that was his way of trying to say that I was indeed claustrophobic, but I disagreed. I had handled being in many other closed spaces before, like MRI machines for a long period of time that did not bother me. I told the nurse that what was bothering me the most was the blue paper on my face and how there had been no air coming in for me to breathe. I was fine now.

After what felt like a very long wait, the doctor finally arrived with the relaxing medicine to be administered. The doctor stuck his head into my enclosure and introduced himself as Dr. Steven. He stated he was placing the port on the right side of my chest because he felt it was the best place for it. I let him know I was right handed, and asked if I was going to be sore, and if it would cause me issues. He let me know it shouldn't be a problem, and that he did a better job when inserting these devices on the right. At that second I felt confident to let him do his best job.

Once the medicine was administered, things went rather quickly. Just as promised, within fifteen minutes the procedure was finished and I was being wheeled back to the room where I had been prepared for surgery. I don't remember much of anything after I received the relaxing medicine.

Amy was waiting for me with a gentle smile. "I'm so proud of you!" she exclaimed, and took my hand. "This was the one thing you were so afraid of, and you did it."

Later that night, I looked up on the internet how an IV port got installed. I was so glad I didn't do this prior to the procedure or I would have requested to be placed under full sedation. I read that a thin, flexible tube called a catheter was run under the skin from the port into a large vein, usually the jugular. Reading this after I already had the procedure sounded even more scary than it had been.

For several days I had discomfort and bruising at the port site. It was very uncomfortable for me to move while lying down in bed. They gave me numbing cream to place on the port one hour prior to any blood draws, hydration, or infusions so I wouldn't feel a thing.

Amy got me home and settled in, and when I finally looked at the clock, I noticed it was after 3:00 p.m. and I still didn't hear from either of my doctors with the results of my PET scan. I decided to reach out to both of their offices and leave messages with their nurses. I knew my mind and emotions could not handle waiting until Monday.

I stated that I was hoping to get the results from the scan today if possible, as it would be brutal to go through another weekend with not knowing. Both nurses told me they would reach out to their respective doctors to see if they had received the results. In the meantime, I rested in bed and waited for their calls.

Around 4:30 p.m. my phone rang, and I answered immediately. The doctor who was calling was not mine, but was the radiation doctor that was in that office that day. "I have good news," she began. "The scan showed that the cancer is limited to inside the anal wall and two lymph nodes in the left groin area. It hadn't spread to any other areas in your body."

I let out a breath I had been holding as tears immediately rolled down my face. "Thank you for taking the time to deliver this good news!" I told the doctor. "This probably sounds strange, I am so happy to hear I have cancer in just those areas of my body. Who wants to say they are happy to have cancer at all?" We both laughed.

Thirty minutes later, I received a call from my chemo doctor with this same news. She said she was so glad that the results came back this way. "Now we can now move forward with treatment Plan 1," Dr. Stephanie said. "Have a wonderful weekend, and I will see you next Wednesday."

Relief spread throughout my body as I set my phone down in bed next to me. All of the stress and tension of these events built up in my chest, and I released all of that energy with a hard, long cry. I thanked God for his comfort, guidance, healing, and words during my PET scan.

Even though I trusted what I felt and I had a sense of comfort and knowing, I also knew that my humanness and ego came out to play. My emotions and my mind got in the way as I played out all of the what-ifs, and that had taken a huge toll on me. When I visited with my children and drove back and forth to appointments with Amy, I had tried my best not to show these feelings. I wanted to stay strong and tell others that I was just fine. I realized then, however, that as I moved forward with my treatment, it wasn't going to be healthy for me to do this alone.

That night when I was curled on the couch, my dog Layla came over to my chest and started sniffing where my port was put in. She knew that something was going on and that something different was in my body. Usually she gave me a hug, she laid her head on my chest under or next to my neck. Tonight's hug was different; she sniffed for a moment and then placed her head right on my port. I felt she was trying to comfort the area that was giving me pain.

During the night, I woke up several times to Layla crying. It wasn't the normal sound of a dog crying in its sleep; Layla deliberately put her head on my chest and cried. I stroked her head and told her I was going to be okay. Did she know something that I didn't know? It was rather concerning, because her embrace felt like she was hugging me like it may be her last time. I started to cry with her. In that unforgettable moment, I felt her embrace, her worry, and her unconditional love.

From that night on, Layla slept on my bed. I placed her bed on top of mine. She started off sleeping in her bed and always ended up sleeping next to me with her head next to mine on the pillow. This was the beginning of a special bond. I knew I would never forget her cry, and in my heart, I held and cherished the love and affection she showed me.

Now that I had my results and knew the plan of attack for this beast inside of me, it was time to reach out and share my situation with those I wanted in my inner circle. I didn't realize how difficult it would be to get the words out. Each time I sat down in a quiet place to make a call, I'd start with, "I have to share something with you," which was then followed with the silence of me crying and struggling to explain everything.

One friend in particular related to how hard it was to voice something tragic over the phone. He shared that this happened to him when he lost his son and had to make calls to his family. His brother had taken this heavy burden off of him and made some of the calls for him. He offered to do the same for me by making a couple of calls to people that were our mutual friends. I gratefully accepted his offer, and when I did, it was like a huge weight had been lifted off my chest. I was so grateful for this act of kindness that he did for me.

"Debra," my friend added that day on the phone. "It's time for us to build an army around you. You have people in your life that love you, who are strong, and who you have helped. We will build your army with people here on earth and with those on the other side, too."

His words were so powerful, and they impacted the way I walked and acted from that day on.. I would have my army around me at all times to lean on, to give me strength, to count on, and to know I was not doing this alone. My entire being felt comforted by this, as if I had just received a huge hug from the inside out. It meant everything to know that I could have this embrace anytime. I could receive one from Spirit, God, and or from my physical family and friends here; all I had to do was ask.

I shared my true, raw feelings with those who I felt could handle hearing me speak this way, while keeping in mind that I needed to always refocus my thoughts into positive ones. I was reminded how important it was to have people to talk to. I surrounded myself and built my army with people who supported me, brought me strength, joy, laughter, comfort, peace, and love during exasperating and painful times.

5

FACING MY NEW REALITY

A my and I met with a nurse for chemo teaching the next day. I was so glad that Amy came with me because we were bombarded with so much information. The nurse gave us sheets with a monthly calendar to enter my upcoming appointments for the next six weeks. She went over the chemo pills that I would be taking, and how to take them twelve hours apart from one another. If I missed a dose, I was told to skip it and wait for the next one.

The nurse questioned us both to make sure we were on the same page: my mock treatment would take place the following week, and my actual treatments would begin on Thursdays along with my first IV infusion. It was explained that a mock treatment would involve going to both locations with my chemo and radiation doctors. At that time they would run through a fake treatment to show me what I would be going through daily.

As the nurse rattled off all my different appointments, medications, infusions, and blood work, I couldn't help but interrupt her. "I'm sorry," I began, "but this all sounds very hard to manage. At least I'll still be able to find joy through this all by continuing to do my gardening. I'll make sure to be careful not to do it in the sun."

She gave me a concerned look and shook her head. "Unfortunately, one of the side effects of chemo is hand-foot syndrome. That's a skin rash that involves swelling, redness, pain, and sometimes peeling of the skin on your palms and the soles of your feet. You may not do any gardening or use any gardening tools once you start treatment. Your skin will be very tender. The tools could crack your skin, leaving you with open sores."

Sadness rushed over me, but I gave the nurse a determined smile anyway. "Well," I began, "treatment starts tomorrow, which means I have only today left to get my roses bushes and plants trimmed." I knew that if I gave myself a deadline, I would be motivated to accomplish this goal without fail.

As soon as I got home, I changed into shorts and grabbed my trimming tools. I went out to trim every bush that needed it so that during the next six weeks I would not have to look outside wishing I would have taken the time to do this. I knew it would drive me crazy not being able to do something that needed to be done. I finished cutting back nine rose bushes, three small palm trees, and four small bushes around my pool before it was dark. Everything was now good until summer. I could sit back, relax, and wait for my roses to bloom.

After thinking over everything I'd learned at the doctor' office that day, I made the decision to not drive to any of my appointments. This wasn't only because of the emotional support I would need, but also because I would be in an altered state from chemo. I didn't want to take any risk of not being able to think correctly or having any delayed reactions when driving that could cause an accident, putting others or myself in danger.

This was going to take some work to organize, as I had no family in town except for my seventeen year old daughter who was in high school. That evening I decided it was time to work with my kids to see when they each would be able to come out and help me. I hesitated each time I picked up my phone; being an independent person, it was not easy for me to ask others for help, especially my children. In my eyes, I didn't know how this was going to work.

When my children came to visit me, it was their time to relax and let Mom take care of them. Now the tables were going to be reversed. *Can I do this?*

I had to give permission to myself to honor myself and my body. It was time for me to allow others to take care of me so that I could rest in order for my body to heal. I was so overwhelmed with all the information, my doctor appointments, and even trying to accept that my life was changing. I knew I could not be involved with coordinating all the details of who could come help me and when they could arrive.

Layla and I were cuddled on the sofa, and I reached over her to decisively pick up my phone. I put a group text together with my kids that included my sister, because she had reached out several times asking when she could come out to help. After taking a deep breath, I typed out a message saying I needed help getting to and from my many appointments, but I would not need them right away.

The responses that came in told me this made my family feel helpless. I also told them I had direct orders, I was not allowed to be around children, because they carried so many germs. This could be difficult, as two of my children had young families they couldn't leave at home alone.

In this case, I was sure to ask them to please place their families first. After looking over my new appointment calendars, I let them know that I felt I would need to have someone with me starting in about a month at the end of March through the middle of April. In the meantime, I would get friends and neighbors to help me for the first month with driving, grocery shopping, and being with me if I needed someone.

For the first time in my life, I was not in control of what was happening in my body or how I was going to feel from upcoming treatments given to my body. I had to surrender to the fact that I no longer had the control. I was ready to do my best and let go, giving God the control, knowing He had a plan for me. I was no longer in the driver's seat: God was. I only wished I knew what His plan was.

When one is facing death, life becomes more valuable. There are common sayings like "live life to the fullest" and "live, laugh, love." I thought I was accomplishing all of this, but who was I kidding? Now that I wasn't sure how much life was left to live, I realized that I had many things I wanted to accomplish. What used to be important to me was no longer important.

I started questioning God: where did this cancer come from? What was the root cause of this? Did I really need another lesson? Hadn't I learned enough through my father's suicide, my mother's illness, my divorce, two near-death accidents by car, and one out of body near-death experience from an illness?

I was a healer that helped many people with their illnesses, so why would I get the challenge of cancer? Could I heal this myself? I had so much compassion for everyone that I healed, so how much more do I need to face? Did I need doctors to help heal me? Was I going to be okay financially? Would my health insurance pay for all of these big medical bills? Was it okay to do healings when I was going through treatments? What healing could I do to help my own healing process? *God,* I prayed. *Please guide me. I will listen and trust my inner guidance from you.*

The other times I faced death, I was given a choice to come back. Was I given a choice now with having cancer? Did my soul plan agree to all of these major, life-changing hardships that I knew I needed to endure before I came here? If my soul knew this plan, then do I have access to it?

These are all answers and lessons I hoped I would receive from God through these grewling treatments. They would all become a huge part of my healing.

I never would have thought that chemo and radiation would be a part of my own inner healing process. I was beginning to see how doctors and God truly worked together hand in hand.

The following day, I reached out to my assistant, Valerie. I knew I needed to come up with a scheduling plan for her. She was receiving many requests for sessions and wasn't sure how she should reply. She knew what I was going through, and told me she would put things on hold until I knew more.

The doctors had given me an estimation of what I was going to experience in the next six weeks, stating that each person's body reacted differently to treatment. Mondays would be my longest days, as I would have to go to both facilities, one for radiation and another for lab work, plus visiting with Dr. Stephanie. From the time I left my house to the time I would return home, about four hours of my day would be gone. Therefore, on Mondays I knew there would be no time left to do a session, and I would most likely not have any energy left to give.

When I had asked God if it's okay to do healings while I was going through treatments, in prayer I heard, "you can continue to do your healings and readings. When you connect, you are not using your body; you are using your soul. The only time you use your body is when you are feeling the pain of what others are experiencing. Communicate with your higher self, your soul, and trust the guidance that you will receive for your human limitations. At some point, you will need to take the time to honor yourself and your body so that you can heal."

I decided to meditate, and removed my ego, placing my humanness aside and asking my higher self for guidance. I didn't receive the answers in a direct format, but I did receive a sense of "knowing" that all was going to be well, and I was going to be able to do this. I felt a sense of calmness go through me. I also felt an emotional strength that I didn't have before, which now pushed me to call Valerie right away.

As I looked over my calendar with Valerie, I knew exactly what needed to be done. The "knowing" I received was the download of information I needed to update my work schedule for the next six weeks during treatment, and for the month of May after my treatments were finished. I had no doubts or second guessing as everything became very clear to me.

A major goal that I wanted to complete during this time period was finishing my book "Proof of Miracles". My goal was to complete the work with my editor, get the manuscript to a publisher for the inside formatting of the book, work with a designer to create the cover, and have the book in print by March 21st.

It was a huge task to finish all of this in twenty-four days even under healthy circumstances, but I was up for the challenge. I also had a strong "knowing" within that this needed to be done. I remembered what I heard in a vision: "You need to finish your book, as this will leave your legacy. Get this done now!"

On March 21st I would be a guest speaker on Suzanne Giesemann's radio show on Unity FM Online radio, called "Messages of Hope". On this show, I would like to announce the title of my book and that it was available for purchase. The show would be about me sharing the true stories of healing and miracles that I wrote about in this book.

Valerie expressed that she felt comfortable with this plan, knowing that if any unexpected circumstances arose during my treatments, she would be able to move my sessions around.

I was so grateful for God's words of guidance. Trusting in this, we both put our actions into place. While praying that day, I consciously removed my fear of the unknown and placed it into God's hands, giving Him full control. When I did this, I received a calmness and a sense of peace within.

I was learning how to work with my doctors and with God. I knew I would continue to see my doctors and go through my treatments, but I would also connect with God daily. Asking God to guide me through each step was a vital piece of what I knew I'd endure over the next six weeks. It also gave me comfort knowing I had a great team of doctors whom I fully trusted and leaned on whenever I had questions or concerns.

I let go of all my fears and let God take over, knowing this was His plan now. "Let go and let God" because He had a plan for me. He was now the one in the driver's seat, and I'd learn what his plan was in the upcoming months.

On Mock Treatment Day, Amy was once again by my side as we set out. Our day started at the Virginia G. Piper Cancer Center and ended at the Arizona Care for Cancer, both located in Scottsdale. The Piper Cancer Center was thirty minutes from my home, and we had another thirty minute drive to the next.

As we drove, I glanced over at my friend and felt an overwhelming wave of gratitude. I realized God knew what he was doing when he placed Amy into my life. She was an angel at my side that gave me strength when I needed it. She was my sounding board when I was listening to the doctors, as I was not able to retain everything all at once. She could turn anything that seemed negative to positive.

We met with Dr. Stephanie first, who gave us the layout of what would happen and where to go tomorrow. I would have my first labs drawn out of my port. She prescribed some numbing medication to place over the port area an hour prior to any infusions or blood draws. This meeting went very easy and rather quick, and afterward we drove over to the cancer center to meet with Dr. Steven.

When we arrived, they had me lay on the radiation table. My body was aligned with where they wanted the radiation beams to come down. Then they placed three markers on my body, one on each side of my hips and one in the center of my lower pelvic area. One of the technicians used a permanent black marker to these spots, then put a small, round sticker over the marker to protect it from fading. I was told that this allowed for identification of target and normal tissue structures using axial CT images. These facilitated improved accuracy, delivery, and dose quantifications.

One of the nurses came up to me. "Debra," she began, "these markers will stay in place for the entire six weeks of treatment. We'll monitor them when we see you, and if they look like they're about to fall off, we'll replace them."

I nodded, as this made sense to me.

"Also," she added, "you won't be able to submerge this area in water; no baths or pools, because we don't want these stickers to come off or for the marker to be erased. It would be almost impossible to find the exact location again, and we need to make sure the radiation beams are being administered in the same location."

"Well, I'm glad it's not pool weather yet," I replied, "but I am a bit disappointed about the bath situation. Guess I'll just save on my water bill, right?"

The nurse smiled at me and nodded. "Good attitude," she replied. "Now, you can take showers, but you'll need to pat the markers gently when drying off. If it's all too much for you, some patients go and get their marks tattooed on them instead."

I stared at her, not sure if this was a joke. "Oh my gosh!" I exclaimed when I realized she was serious. "No way. That's a constant reminder that I don't want to have, and definitely don't want to explain to others. I'll just be careful with these dots.

The nurses positioned my body once more, and then told me to not move so they could do all of the work. It was a weird feeling, as I naturally wanted to help them move my body as they shifted me to the left or right. It was extremely important that my body was positioned just right so that the radiation beams would hit this exact area each time, and they informed me that I would have to be positioned like this over the next thirty treatments.

When I was back with Amy, I looked once again over at her calm face. "You know," I began as we arrived back at her car. "This is so unreal, isn't it?"

"Yeah," she agreed with a nod. "We should be out hiking together right now, not going to cancer centers learning about cancer treatments."

The reality set in for both of us as we started back toward my home. Tomorrow the real deal would begin. Amy must have noticed the worry in my eyes, because she said, "Debra, you should take this one day at a time. Don't get consumed with what may or may not come."

I nodded, comforted by her words. "You're right. All of the unknowns will be revealed each day." I knew it was time for me to walk through this with as much grace as I could.

When I got home and made my way to my front door, I noticed my neighbor Larry out in his yard.. I waved and went over to chat with him, since he already knew a little about my situation. "This year didn't start on a good note," I sighed.

Larry gave me a funny look. "Yes, it did Debra," he replied. "It's a miracle you found this so that it could be cured."

"Perfectly said!" I agreed, glad to hear such a positive perspective. I held onto those words, knowing I wouldn't forget them. It was a miracle!

It was time for me to start my healing process.

6

———◆———

MY PUSH DAY

W hen I woke up, my first thoughts were on my nine chemo pills. I was nervous about how they were going to make me feel, so I decided to answer a few emails and then take my shower.

In my office, I sat at my desk and looked over my inbox. I saw one from my editor letting me know the editing process for "Proof of Miracles" was complete! What a perfect way to start the day. My first goal had been met, and now I could start my treatments knowing that this was finalized and ready to be sent to my publisher. I responded back with so much gratitude for her completing this so quickly. If she only knew all the reasons why it meant so much to me. I felt like I was on cloud nine as I walked into my bathroom to take my shower.

After my shower, I placed some numbing medicine around and on my port, and covered it with saran wrap. I then returned to my bedroom where I stood to pray. *I need to remove all of my fear and become friends with my medicine and with my port,* I thought. I sat in my comfy, over-sized white chair where the morning sun came through my window.

I felt that whatever I believed and spoke my body would listen to. Words and thoughts were energy that my body would feel. I needed to keep these thoughts positive. I also needed to replace all my thoughts of fear with love. Fear would continue to destroy my body as love would heal my body.

Knowing that something was missing, I went to my kitchen in search of something that I could place my medicine on. I wanted to be able to hold each dose in my hands and raise them up in prayer for God to bless. I was guided to the cabinet that held my nice dishes. As soon as I opened the cabinet, I knew right away which piece I needed.

I took out a small, round plate that was light blue with white dragonflies. I purchased these tiny plates in memory of my father. He used the dragonfly to get my attention and let me know he was with me. This was perfect! My father was letting me know that he would be at my side each and every time I would take my chemo pills. *Thanks, Dad,* I thought as I made my way back to my place of prayer in my bedroom. *Thank you for guiding me to this plate.*

MY PRAYER FOR CHEMO PILLS

Once I had gathered my medicine, I closed my eyes and took a deep, cleansing breath for a moment. Then, with two hands, I held each of my pills on the dragonfly plate in front of a picture of Jesus that hung on my wall. "Dear Heavenly Father," I began quietly, "I place this medicine in front of you for you to bless."

As always, I felt the presence of God through the eyes of the picture. "Please alter this medicine for my body, so that I will have no side effects from this medicine, and that this medicine will destroy what my body does not need. Let it heal the illness that is in my body, destroying, disintegrating, and taking this illness out of me now. Thank you, God, for this medicine that I am about to receive. I love this medicine, as it was made to heal me. I now remove any fear of this medicine, giving you full control. I trust the plan you have for me."

I held my dragonfly plate in one hand and took two pills off at a time to digest. Each time I lifted them up in front of my Jesus picture for God to bless before I would digest. After I digested my last pill, I said, "Thank you, God. Amen."

My 4 X 4 inch Dragonfly Plate

My morning was going by fast, and I went over to my closet to get dressed for this big day. As I browsed through drawers and rows of hangers, I decided that I needed to dress in clothes with an army pattern on them. This would represent that my army was going with me and standing by my side. My army consisted of all my family and friends here on earth that I told about this cancer, my loved ones in Spirit, and God. I would walk with strength, courage, and gratitude for what I was about to receive through the doctors, nurses, my medicine, and God.

I heard Amy's knock at my front door and knew it was time. Even though my doctors told me what to expect, I really had no idea what I was about to face emotionally, physically, and spiritually.

The morning of my first day of all treatments. I wore my army pants.

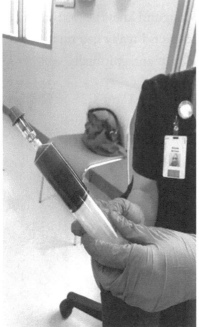 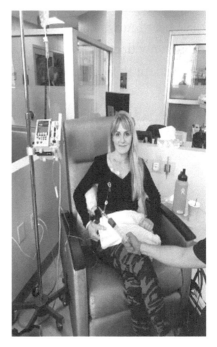

Mitomycin-C (IV Chemo) Day 1   IV injection going into my port

When we entered the Piper Cancer Center, my heart raced. My nerves were running high as I signed in and was told I needed to go down to the lab center to get my blood drawn. My doctor wanted to see my platelet count before I received my infusion. This was my first time having anything drawn out of my port, and I wondered what it was going to feel like.

"Okay, Debra," a nurse said to me once I was situated in the chair in a small, white room I was becoming too comfortable with. "Go ahead and take a deep breath." When I did, she inserted the needle into the port in my chest.

I winced when I felt a big pinch and a burning sensation. After the blood was drawn, she again asked me to take a deep breath in, then pulled the needle out. It happened so quickly and I was so relieved it was over that I didn't remember how it felt coming out. The doctor received my results within minutes, and I was informed that my plate-let count came in at 273, which was an acceptable range for me to be clear for the treatment that day.

When I finished with my lab work, I took the elevator up to the second floor where Dr. Stephanie's office was. As Amy and I waited for the nurse to bring us back to the infusion center, I noticed there were many wigs displayed in glass cases at the front of the room. A wave of gratitude washed over me at that moment, knowing this could be much worse.

I was led by a nurse into the infusion center, down a series of halls that were filled with silence. Then, in front of me were rows of people sitting in chairs as they received their chemo treatments. I noticed that there were some patients in a different room that extended off from the main one, and these people looked very sick and weak. Some had lost their hair, some wore wigs, and some didn't. I took all of this in with a quick glance, trying my best not to be overwhelmed.

I recalled that Dr. Stephanie said I should plan on being in the in-fusion chair for about an hour and a half. It took fifty minutes for the nurses to receive the Mitomycin-C treatment and around ten minutes to inject the medicine and the rest of the time was waiting for the rest of the fluids to go through my port. The fluids were for hydration and to help flush all the Mitomycin through the veins and into the body.

As I waited in my chair for the nurses to receive the Mitomycin-C, I looked at the woman who sat next to me. She was at least sixty years old, and wore a short, white wig. She gave me a kind smile and intro-duced herself, then her son who sat with her.

"Is this your first time?" she asked, and when I nodded, she con-tinued, "Today is my seventh and final infusion. And my last. My son here has come to every one with me."

It was so endearing to see how supportive her son was, and I told her as much. I was trying my best to be brave as the nurse came back to inject my medicine, but I wasn't sure how well it showed. I didn't feel anything during the injection; there was no burning sensation, and no nausea. The nurse told me it was time to wait while they ran fluids through my port to help flush the medicine through my body.

"You know," began the woman next to me, "you'll get through this. You'll be okay. God bless you."

I felt tears touch my eyes, momentarily overwhelmed by her sweet words. It wasn't long till her treatment was finished and suddenly all the nurses gathered around her. They threw confetti in the air to celebrate her completion day, and everyone hugged as tears were shed. The bond between this elderly woman and the staff had created on her journey was strong and touching to witness.

A bit of hope sparked in my heart, and I wondered if I would be as strong as her on my last day. My gaze drifted over to the private rooms that housed the weaker patients, reminding myself that things could be much worse. I couldn't help my racing thoughts and I recalled that I could be living with my sons right now, going through a much more intense treatment plan.

I was happy to be where I was and grateful for the plan God gave me.

When I was finished with the infusion, it was time to head over the next clinic to have my first radiation treatment. I was led back to a large, dark room that was dominated by a huge machine. Seeing it for the first time was intimidating and frightening. The nurses told me I needed to undress from my waist down, but I could keep my underwear on.

As I lay on the table, they positioned my body so that the radiation beams would hit the three markers that were on my body, triggering the area that needed to be treated. I was told not to move the entire time and to keep my hands up on my chest. The nurse then pressed a button that raised and moved the table toward the radiation machine. After it was set in place, the nurses left the room.

At first, the machine moved close to me, then the sides came inward to take images of my body. After that was complete, it moved above me and started its rotations. From my still position, I watched as it rotated from above me to underneath the table, making a complete rotation three times. The entire process from set up to completion took about fifteen minutes. I remembered that radiation is a form of electromagnetic energy, such as x-rays and electrons. It had the ability to interact with the cancer cells and limit the cell's ability to reproduce and grow.

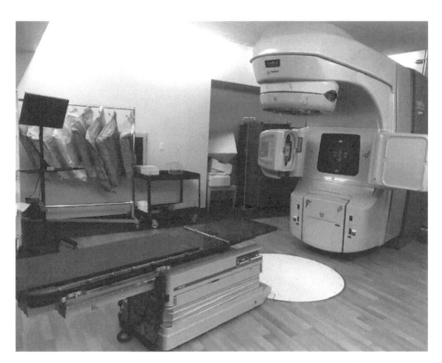

The radiation machine that I would receive radiation from for 30 days

I didn't feel anything from this treatment, but I was beginning to feel exhausted. The emotional stress of everything I'd gone through that day began to weigh heavily on me. All of the unknowns with how my treatments would feel and work were revealed. I was ready to go home.

I spent the rest of the day resting, and I was sure to drink plenty of fluids and eat lots of protein. That night, I took my final treatment of the day of nine chemo pills, saying my prayer before taking each one. I went to bed thanking God and my army for helping me get through my first day.

7

REPLACING FEAR WITH FAITH

After breakfast, I said my prayer while taking my nine chemo pills and then went for my second radiation treatment in the afternoon. I had a different feeling walking into the radiation room today. I was no longer fearful of what I was facing. The nurse asked if I wanted a blanket to stay warm. As she placed the white blanket on my body, I thanked her with tears running from my eyes. I felt the compassion she had for me, and she didn't even know me that well yet. As I lay on the table and the nurses left, I decided that it was time that I would embrace this large machine.

FROM THEN ON, I WHISPERED THIS PRAYER DURING
MY RADIATION TREATMENTS:

"Thank you, God, for this machine that is sending radiation to the areas that I need healed. I accept this radiation and love this machine that you helped create. God, please guide the radiation to only the areas that are needed and protect all areas of my body that do not need it. Destroy, disintegrate, and remove the cancer from my body."

I kept my eyes closed, feeling the heaviness of the blanket and the warmth that surrounded me. This feeling represented that

God's white light (my white blanket) holding me and God's love running through me (the warmth) and with me during the entire treatment.

That night after I said my prayer and took my nine chemo pills, I felt a strength in me that didn't exist before I started my treatments. Embracing my medicine and now the radiation machine with love and prayers was helping me know that God was at my side through each and every treatment. I removed my fear and replaced it with love. God is love, and love heals.

As I got ready for bed and cuddled up with Layla, I remembered how blessed I was to have no radiation treatments or chemo pills to take during the weekends. I was especially grateful for this weekend after being heavily doused with so much chemo at once.

I wasn't feeling any effects from my first day of treatments. The doctors told me after receiving the Mitomycin injection that it may take a few days for me to feel the effects of this medicine combined with the chemo pills and radiation.

When I woke, however, I didn't know what hit me. I felt drugged, dizzy, and very weak,. I was home alone and Layla needed to be taken outside. I sat on the floor putting on her leash, but with the way my head was spinning, I didn't know if I could walk outside without fainting.

I decided I needed to call my oldest son, so I Facetimed him. I felt that seeing him and hearing his voice would help give me the strength I needed. He was always so positive and encouraging. I also wanted him with me in case I did faint so he could call on one of my neighbors for help.

As soon as Steven answered the phone, tears began to run down my face. "This is so hard," I cried. "I didn't think this was going to take me down this violently. What am I going to do if I can't even take the dog outside?"

"Calm down, Mom," he said, trying to reassure me. "We can do this together."

With my phone in one hand and Layla's leash in the other, I balanced myself against the wall and opened the door before slowly proceeding to walk outside. I drew on every bit of my strength to keep one foot in front of the other.

I made it about twenty steps to the gravel for Layla to pee. I didn't think I was going to be able to stand much longer, and I didn't want to sit or fall on the rocks. I glanced over to my grass on the far side of my yard. Once I made it there, I collapsed on the grass bawling.

Weaknesses, dizziness, and extreme nausea overwhelmed me. Compared to how I had felt yesterday, this was the lowest I had been emotionally, physically, and spiritually. I never in a thousand years imagined this could be so debilitating. The doctors told me this was going to hit me and that I would be extremely exhausted. I realized then that they were not kidding! I felt like I had lost all of my strength.

Layla was worried and kept coming over to console me. Eventually she did her business and I took my time getting us back into the house safely.

I went to the couch and sat down. My body was shaking and I was still very emotional. Steven had been watching how weak I was and was talking me through my mental break down.

"Mom," he said now, and I tried my best to steady my shaking hand so I could see his concerned face on my screen. "You need to call one of your friends or your neighbors to come sit with you. Do you want me to come out today to take care of you?"

"My doctors warned me this was going to happen," I said. "I should feel better by Monday or Tuesday. Besides, you should save the time for later dates when I'll need you more."

I didn't want anyone to come for the first three weeks of my treatments. I was told the next three weeks I would feel tired, but that I would still be able to work full time if needed. Steven understood, but I could tell he didn't feel comfortable until I promised I would call someone to come over to be with me as soon as we hung up.

I called my neighbor Patty and she was over within minutes. She had a key to the front door and also knew the garage code so I would not have to get up to let her in. The thought of having to try and answer the door seemed completely unmanageable.

Once Patty saw how bad of shape I was in, she didn't leave my side. We sat on the couch together, crying and watching endless amounts of TV shows. When the light faded outside the windows and night began to fall, she helped get me into bed, took Layla out, and said she would keep her phone next to her throughout the night. If I needed anything, I shouldn't hesitate to call her.

That night before I went to sleep, in my prayers I asked God to help guide my family on which days they should come out to take care of me. I had to let go and trust that God heard my request. All would turn out just the way it was meant to be.

After Steven saw how hard of a time I had that day, he took immediate action and began coordinating with his siblings and my sister to figure out when everyone could contribute to helping me.

The following day, I woke up to Patty crying at my bedside. She grabbed my hands and held them sobbing she told me that she had been texting and calling me but wasn't getting any response. She felt so bad waking me up and coming over unannounced. She was worried that I may have taken Layla outside and fell where I was not able to call for help. She was so relieved to see that I was okay and still in bed.

I was so touched by Patty's concern and love for me. Her reactions showed me how bad I really was yesterday, and I realized how blessed I was to have Patty right across the street from me. My children felt the same way. They had someone to reach out to at anytime to get updates on me, or to hear from someone else how I truly was doing.

My children all quickly coordinated when they would visit me over the next couple of months, with Stephanie making a calendar to make sure I was never left alone. With this plan, I would have three weeks on my own and then four and a half weeks with someone helping me. Dates were arranged and flights were booked.

Though I could feel their love and concern, I didn't know how I was going to handle others taking care of me, especially my own children. Usually when they came to visit, it was my job as Mom to do all the work so they could relax and enjoy. This was going to be a challenge that I would have to undertake. I wondered if I would be able to do this, or if I would push myself to do things that I shouldn't be doing like cooking and cleaning.

Over the first three weeks, my neighbors and a few friends always made sure to check on me to see if I needed anything. One friend in particular went out of his way to take me to his butcher to buy fresh chicken, homemade chicken broth, and farm fresh eggs. He also took me to his favorite seafood butcher to purchase some fresh fish that was flown in from all around the world.

If I ran out of any of these items and wanted more, he offered to pick them up and deliver them to me. He did not live close by, so this was very kind of him. He even bought me an egg maker from Amazon and had it delivered to my house. When he brought me eggs, he cooked them, peeled them, and placed them in a bag for me for the week. This reminded me that the things that our friends did made life easier in hard times, but it also let me know how much I mattered to them. It showed me how many people loved me.

I received one of the kindest and most thoughtful gifts from Amy's daughter, Erin. Erin was on her college spring break, but she took the time out of her busy travel schedule to make me a beautiful calendar. Along with it, she gave me star stickers to place on each day after I completed my treatments. I placed this on my kitchen counter for me to see daily.

I didn't realize how much this calendar was going to do for me mentally. It gave me strength seeing that I was getting through this, one day at a time. It also gave me comfort in knowing how many treatments were left. At the beginning of each week, I told myself, "you can do this." At the end of the week, I said, "you completed another week, Debra. Good job." This began a ritual for me.

Placing stickers on my calendar was like rewarding myself for getting through each day. Seeing the stars in a row telling me how many days I'd completed gave me hope and the knowledge that I could do this. My countdown had begun.

My days were long, and I often wondered how I was going to get through six full weeks. That's when I heard my mother in spirit say to me, "I went through thirteen years of pain and suffering. You can do six weeks."

These words really impacted me. I felt shameful for doubting myself so much. How could I complain after my mother went through so much more? I knew my mother was not being stern and that she was coming from a place of love. Her words gave me renewed strength, knowing that she was right. This was six weeks, not my entire life. These six weeks wouldn't be easy and would seem long, but once I completed them, they would be behind me.

It took my entire first weekend to recover from my extreme fatigue, dizziness, and nausea left over from the events of my Push Day. I was given a nausea medicine that I could take as needed every eight hours. I used this and it helped so tremendously that I decided to keep it close by for any time I felt nauseous. The bottle sat next to my chemo pills as a reminder where I wouldn't forget them.

Amy was my main driver for the next three weeks, and when she wasn't able to Patty took over. One particular day they were both unavailable, so my dear friend Lynn came to my rescue. This was a huge undertaking for anyone; Mondays were a four hour turn-around, and the other four days in the week took two and a half hours. I scheduled all of my appointments for later in the afternoon so that I could work in the morning, and so these ladies had some time in their day to accomplish whatever they needed.

On Sunday, March 3rd, I turned in my manuscript of my book "Proof of Miracles" to a publisher for the interior formatting. She lived out of the country, so our time differences would either work against us or for us.

My goal now was to work with her to finalize all the editing inside the book that would make it beautiful. I chose the fonts for the book and for the chapter headers, the alignment of each page, placed the pictures properly, added page numbers, and picked the symbol that I wanted to use behind the chapter number that would go next to each chapter title. Knowing the length of the book, I decided to have it printed on white paper. If I chose to print in cream, the paper was thicker and cause the binding to be even bigger.

Now that I had accomplished all of this, I contacted the person that would be designing the front and back covers for the book.

Despite everything else going on, I was motivated to get this completed and published on Amazon before my radio show with Suzanne Giesemann on March 21st. That gave us two and a half weeks, not to mention that I also needed a few days to get the book uploaded.

This was a big goal to get finished in such a short period of time. I asked God for his hand and favor to help get this book finished on time. I was doing what I heard in my vision: "You need to finish your book, as this will leave your legacy. Get this done now!"

These words gave me a lot of strength to accomplish this goal. It felt like a competition between me and my body. I had to get this done, not only before the radio show that I was going to be on; I also knew I was getting this finished before I would become too sick to do anything.

Working hard to finish my book by this date gave me something to focus on rather than focusing on how I was feeling. It gave me a purpose.

Four days after my Big Push Day, I started experiencing some of the side effects from the Mitomycin infusion and chemo pills. I was beginning to have the hand-foot syndrome that my doctor mentioned. The skin on the palms of my hands became very tight, and the skin on my fingers was tender to the touch. I began putting Aquaphor ointment on my hands and feet at night, usually an hour before I went to bed. After I lubricated them well, I put gloves on my hands and socks on my feet to help keep them moist so they wouldn't crack. I often wanted to text someone, but remembered I couldn't with the gloves. On the first day it became such a nuisance that I ended up cutting the fingertips off of the gloves.

I decided that my original work schedule wasn't going to work. I wanted to play it safe, knowing that I would feel good for the next two weeks. I decided to have Valerie move all my healing and reading sessions that were scheduled for the last two weeks of March and place them into the first two weeks of March on days that were open. Since I only did one session per day, I needed to work both of these Saturdays to fit everyone in.

I prayed that if this was what God wanted me to do, everything would fall into place just as God wanted it to be. Valerie did an amazing job rescheduling the sessions. I ended up not moving two of my sessions; one was for the third week and one was for the fourth week of March. These had been scheduled a month in advance. I felt I was being guided, and that I would be okay because there was only one per week. I trusted in this plan and new God would guide each step of the way.

I settled into my office for my reading session that Monday morning, and I was blown away by how clear Spirit came through. It felt like I was hearing all of their messages as clearly as I would if I was talking to them over the phone. I gave gratitude to God for giving me this awareness. I was being shown that Spirit could work through me at anytime, no matter what was going on in my life or in my body. I had a few hours to rest before Amy would pick me up to take me to my radiation treatment.

When I arrived, the nurses asked me how I felt after my Big Push Day last Thursday. I admitted that it was tougher than I could have ever imagined. It kicked my butt! I was glad that the side effects had lessened so that I could be with them that day.

When I returned home, I spent the remainder of my day resting. My body was exhausted from my treatment that day. I grabbed something light for dinner out of my refrigerator and called it an early night.

One week since I started my chemo pills and had my first infusion, Amy took me to get my labs drawn. They showed that my platelet count was at 148, which was much lower from my first set of labs on February 14th, the first day I met Dr. Stephanie, when they were at 273.

My platelet count of 148 was considered to be in the good range to continue chemo. The normal range for a healthy person was 130-450, and anything under a count of 100 meant we would need to stop treatments. It was important for the doctors to watch my platelet counts, as this would let them know how my body was tolerating the chemo.

Dr. Stephanie had informed me that chemo would destroy my cells, especially those in my bone marrow that produced platelets. I knew that a low platelet count could lead to serious blood loss.

Because I did have a lower blood count, I was told not to do heavy lifting and to avoid cutting my nails. I couldn't shave with a razor or use household tools such as knives or scissors. My doctor warned me not to blow my nose forcefully, as it may cause nose bleeds. I had to watch for bruising on my arms or legs with or without injury. I was to be careful at all times.

I still had plenty of energy to get my normal daily tasks done, but I started having my youngest daughter do a few of my errands, like picking up my mail at my post office box and picking up a few items at the grocery store here and there. This was important so that I wouldn't compromise my immune system by being around others that may have a cold.

This was a big undertaking for a seventeen year old who was busy going to school, doing her homework, working, and trying to have her own time for socializing. Allison started seeing her friends outside of the house to protect me. This was hard, as the kids usually hung out here. They started spending time at coffee houses and or meeting at restaurants for lunch or dinner. This ended up working out well, as Allison was able to take a break from what was going on at home.

I was worried about her emotional status and didn't want my challenge with cancer to cause her to have any problems with her school work. Whenever she brought in my mail or chatted with me while unloading some groceries, I saw the stress Allison was holding onto. It didn't take long for me to pick up my phone one evening and text her to ask if she would like to speak with her counselor at school. Her immediate response was yes.

Allison shared with me that her teachers saw that something was wrong when she would break down crying in her classes or even when walking down the hallways. She couldn't control how frightened she was. She didn't want to lose me.

The counselor was amazing. This woman shared that at Allison's age, her father had gone through cancer. It had been difficult for her at the time, but he was still living today and doing well. This gave Allison hope, and also made her feel safe enough to share her own feelings. Releasing these feelings and hearing this woman's story about her dad helped Allison stay strong and believe that her mom would be okay, too.

Allison's counselor asked her if her mother had any support with family or in the community. My daughter wasn't sure, as all of our family lived out of town. This counselor then went above and beyond her call of duty and reached out to me to see if I had the support I needed, or if there was anything she could do to help me. I told her I had the support, but thanked her for all she did for my daughter. Her compassion was a gift that gave my daughter the comfort she needed at a very difficult time in her life.

With my work, I knew God was guiding me as my healing and readings were spot on and they were not draining me. I gave so much gratitude to God for allowing me to this work. Everything was on task, just as I hoped and prayed it would be.

8

CHALLENGES OF CANCER

On my tenth day of treatment, I received a copy of my book cover. With excitement and pride, I approved the final version of the front and back of my book! Another one of my goals completed on time. This didn't come easy, as it took two times for my designer to come up with a picture that I felt was right.

I felt bad rejecting the first design, but I didn't feel in my heart that it was the right one. After the front cover was finished, we worked together to get all of the words placed on the back cover, and decided on how we wanted the color of the binding laid out. I was beyond pleased with the final version.

Now all I needed was to wait for the final page count of the book from my publisher, and receive the ISBN number from Amazon. These were the final steps left before I could rest easy, knowing "Proof of Miracles" would be published in a way that I was absolutely confident with and proud of.

That night my friends Lynn and Pam were coming over to check on me. They were bringing dinner for us all, and it would be the first time that I would see Pam since I shared what was going on. When they arrived, they embraced me and gave me flowers the second they were through the door.

The three of us had a lovely time hanging out, and eating pizza and salad. They even brought dessert, but we ended up placing it in my freezer for my family when they came to visit. Lynn and Pam were so kind and kept their visit short when they noticed my tiredness was setting in. Before they left, they cleaned all the dishes and made my kitchen look better than it did before they arrived. I went to bed that night full of love. Before drifting off to sleep, I said a prayer, recognizing how blessed I was to have those two wonderful women in my life.

When I began my second week of treatment, I was no longer able to tolerate the smell of any foods. Opening the refrigerator made me puke when I smelled what was inside. My sense of smell was so heightened, and I had never experienced anything like this. Not only could I smell everything and anything, but I also I didn't like any and all of the food that I could smell. If anyone cooked in the house, by the time they were done, I could not eat it.

We started to order takeout dinners from local restaurants. When my daughter was with her dad, my neighbor Larry made me food at his house so that I didn't smell it and brought it down for me to eat. He told me he was worried that I wasn't eating enough, so this way he was able to see that I had something.

"I'm worried about you, Debra," Larry told me one evening. He gave me a concerned look from across my kitchen after setting down a wrapped plate of food. "It's hard watching you go through this."

I was touched by his kindness, knowing he was going out of his way to bring me meals.

"You're losing weight," Larry continued, "and anyone looking at you can see that something's wrong."

"Well, I feel stronger than I look," I tried to reassure him.

"No offense, Deb," Larry replied, "but your face is looking drawn, and I can see how this is impacting your life. Just take it easy, okay?"

Dr. Stephanie called me after she received the results from my labs that I had drawn that afternoon. My platelets had dropped to 109. She was concerned, and let me know she didn't want my count to continue to drop any lower. Therefore, she said I needed to lower my chemo pills from nine pills twice a day to seven pills twice a day. I was also experiencing lots of diarrhea whenever I ate, and she hoped that reducing the pills would help with this issue, too.

After getting off the phone, I went to my office and was delighted to see a message from my designer. The same man who created the beautiful cover of my book had been working on the logo design for my publishing company. All I told him was the title and its meaning: Army for Love, but instead of using the word "for", I wanted to use the number "4". I opened his email and saw that he came back with a design, stating that the circle he put around the number "4" represented being surrounded and loved by your people/your army. I loved it!

I downloaded the design and opened it up so it filled my computer screen. Sitting back in my chair, I thought about how I had been contemplating the name for my publishing company. One day when I was receiving my radiation treatment, after I said my prayers, I started thinking to myself about different names. Within seconds, I heard in my mind the words "Army Four Love."

Usually when words came to me so effortlessly and so quickly, I knew they were given to me from a Higher Source or from Spirit. Once I heard this title, I didn't second guess the name anymore. It was perfect! I thanked Spirit and God for giving me the title. It was when I wrote the words down that I decided I needed to use the number "4" and not the word "for", as a number represented quantity and quantity would represent that one would have many people in one's army. It also was part of my favorite number "44". It couldn't get better than this!

My energy level was low, but when I did my sessions for work, I felt like I was back to my normal, healthy self. I even told Valerie that I wished I could stay in my sessions all day, as I felt my best when I was in a healing session healing others. At some level, I was given this "knowing within" that when I was doing a healing, I was also being healed. I was always in awe of how God worked.

Later that week on my fourteenth day of treatment, I had a hair appointment in the afternoon. I moved my radiation up to early that morning so that I could fit this in. It was nice going into the salon. The last time I was there thirty days ago, I had an extremely hard time, but now my hair stylist would have a chance to see how I was doing. Plus, last time I wondered if I would even be able to sit to have my hair done. I felt so blessed that I was able go now with the bit of energy I had.

When Patty picked me up and we headed to the salon, I realized it seemed like a long time since I was outside of my home doing something for myself besides receiving treatments. Despite how freeing this was, I knew I wouldn't be out that long. I made sure I didn't eat anything hours before so that I wouldn't have any diarrhea.

It was a fear of mine of how horrific it would be if I had to stop my stylist from doing my hair so I could run across the salon in front of everyone to make it to the bathroom on time. This was the main reason I didn't leave my house. If my stomach started to act up, I immediately panicked. Thank goodness, that day I was able to get through my appointment without having any issues.

At the end of the week on St. Patrick's Day, I had been planning for weeks to go to a friend's house to celebrate the holiday and his new home. He invited all of his friends and family, who I was excited to meet. We had some mutual friends that would also be attending. When the day arrived, however, I knew it wasn't in my best interest to go and be around a lot of people when my immune system was low.

I knew he was looking forward to me coming, too, so my heart was broken when I made the call to tell him I could not attend. My friend took pictures to show me all the decorations and the party. He made me feel like I was still part of his day. He also made me feel so much better when he texted saying:

"There is no way you could have walked in my house! The smell of the cooked cabbage is terrible. It would have stopped you at the curb."

Even though this made me laugh, I knew it was true; I would not have been able to handle the smell. I would have made the long drive to his house and had to turn right around. I was so relieved when he shared this with me. This showed me that I truly wasn't meant to go and that I made the right choice.

At the beginning of my third week, my platelet count dropped to a dangerous 60. Even though it was only Monday, I was ordered to stop taking all chemo pills for the remainder of the week. I was going to retest my platelet count the following Monday, and my doctor hoped that I would be able to rebuild my platelets during this time before my last infusion at the end of the month.

Dr. Stephanie also told me that I was not allowed to be around any small children or anyone who was sick. She felt children were a walking petri dish full of germs. There was no way for me to predict when they could break out with a cold or fever, and children were always walking around with many contagious germs. These were especially hard for a person that was receiving chemo and who had a low platelet count like me. She told me that if I was to catch a cold, it would take me down for months and it would be very hard for me to overcome.

She recommended that no one visited me with has a cold, and that I should stay away from grocery stores and crowded places. In fact, it was best if I just stayed home. Everyone that was taking care of me should wash their hands a lot to keep away germs they may get throughout the day.

I asked her when she thought I would have a stronger immune system to see my grandkids. I wanted to give my children a date that we could all hold on to. I also knew that would take some pressure off of myself, because my daughter was pushing to see me. She was really missing me and felt the need to see me to know that I was okay. My doctor responded that she felt that it would be safe to say that I would have my immune system back by the end of July.

That gave me four months of healing.

I knew this news was going to be hard on my daughter, as she was planning on coming out April 18th-22nd with her one and a half year old son. When I shared that she couldn't make this trip, she was heartbroken. She wanted to take care of me and felt it was unfair that her two brothers were able to come but she wasn't. I didn't want to take her away from her son, as I knew it would be hard on her to leave him. The conversation didn't go well.

This was the first time that I had to put myself first and voice my truth. I told Stephanie that this wasn't about how she felt, and that she needed to let me do what I felt was right for me. I had to put my health first. I felt in my heart that I would feel better if she didn't come out to help me. I felt that if she did, it would put more stress on her worrying about her family and their needs, which would then put unnecessary stress on me.

Whenever my children were upset, I felt their energy and tried to help them in any way I could. Right then, however, I couldn't help anyone else but myself. I let Stephanie know that it wasn't easy for me, either; I was losing, too. I didn't get to see her or my grandson.

I shared with her and with my older son that I couldn't see the grandchildren until months after my treatments which the earliest could be mid July. I also stated to them that I didn't want my grandchildren to see me this way. They were used to me playing with them, and right now I couldn't do much of anything, let alone play with my grandkids.

I was feeling very weak and tired, but I was looking forward to my youngest son Brad arriving the next day. This was not only good for me, but I also knew it would be good for Allison to have some help and support. She was helping me cook and pick up the house daily. Sometimes, she even made dinner for herself and then prepared something different for me.

She was such a trooper. I saw that it wasn't easy, but she never complained. She was trying to make my life easier and was always telling me to relax and rest. With all of her love, support, and help I was able to rest the remainder of my day after my treatments.

I saw how God worked behind the scenes to guide my family to visit exactly when I needed them. I was also grateful that I trusted my instincts, that I called God's guidance, to have Valerie move all my sessions to the weeks prior. All was going as God planned.

During the first three weeks of March, I continued to eat a no carb diet with lots of proteins. I was proud with how much I was able to eat, and I was surprised at how full I was without eating any carbs. Usually for breakfast, I had a hard boiled egg, a few pieces of grilled chicken, a banana or blueberries, and some hot tea. At lunch, I ate a grilled chicken breast, a few slices of cheese, fruit, and water. In between meals, I had a cup of homemade chicken bone broth. For dinner, I had another chicken breast with vegetables and some water.

The effects from the radiation during these three weeks were not that bad. I really didn't have any pain at all, but the radiation caused my body to be fatigued. I knew in time that the radiation would get worse due to the cumulative treatments.

One thing I knew from the beginning was that in order to kill cancer, it had to be completely destroyed, and by doing so, everything in my body was being attacked. It was like I was dead inside, but my Spirit was still living.

There were times that my brain felt foggy and I couldn't think the same as I used to. Others who have had cancer told me what I was experiencing what was called "chemo brain." Cancer survivors described this as thinking and memory problems that could occur during and after cancer treatments.

Sometimes, when I was in the middle of a sentence I couldn't bring forth the word that I was trying to say. It would be gone. This was a frustrating and strange feeling. I couldn't remember the simplest words.

Sometimes my friends would just say the missing word for me to help me finish my sentences. I found it interesting, however, that during my healing sessions, this never happened. I never skipped a beat and the words flowed through me. God was showing me how Spirit used my voice to speak through me.

I was able to do the two healing sessions I had scheduled at the end of the month. God continued to show me how He was in control. I kept looking forward to my work, because it lifted my spirits to know God was continuing to use me as his instrument.

I also loved being surrounded in His light and love. As I was healing my clients, God was also raising my vibration and frequency. My body felt stronger. I was receiving more strength to heal myself. As I was giving, I was also receiving.

9

ACCOMPLISHING MY GOALS

Brad, my youngest son, was landing at 9:30 that morning. Because I wasn't able to drive, I had arranged my driver, JT, to handle all airport runs. He took care of picking up and dropping off everyone that came to help me.

While I was preparing my breakfast and getting ready for Brad's arrival, I heard my phone go off on the kitchen counter. Allison's name flashed on the screen, and I opened a text from her that said she had come down with a cough. She was with her dad that weekend, and today was the day she was returning. I knew she was excited to see her brother and anxious to see how I was doing.

I sighed, knowing what I had to say: "Allison," I typed, "You can't come here until your cough is gone, sweetheart. I can't take the risk right now."

It broke my heart to send her this message, but once again I was learning how to put myself first. I had to honor myself, voice the truth, and stand strong with my decision.

"It's just allergies," Allison sent back, almost immediately.

Even though it was hard, I insisted on telling her that because I didn't know what she was fighting, she couldn't come home until she was clear. Needless to say, she was not happy with these words, but respected them as she knew she didn't have a choice.

I made my way to my office to work on the editing for my book, "Proof of Miracles". There were some corrections to the chapter titles, the placing of the symbol next to the title, and the changing of the font on the book title inside the cover to match the same one that was used for the outside.

These were small yet important final pieces that were important to me, and now I was able to double-check all them. I approved the interior designs and signed off on my book. I felt a bit nervous when I glanced at my calendar. I was getting down to the wire with the radio show only two days away.

I heard a car door shut outside, and quickly made my way to the living room to greet Brad as he arrived. He barely made it through my door before I hugged him tightly. We had not seen each other since Thanksgiving. As I held him close, I knew I needed him to help me, but I also wanted this time alone with him.

It had been a long time since I had spent one on one time with any of my children. In that moment, I decided that I was going to use this time as a gift to bond, laugh, share memories, and catch up with Brad about what was going on in his life. If I had to get one positive thing out of my illness, it would be the blessing of spending quality time separately with each of my children.

That day I had hydration at the chemo center, then we would be heading to the other center for radiation. My body was becoming dehydrated from the chemo, which was a common side effect. Chemotherapy could rob the body of fluids and electrolytes, which was a serious concern. I was feeling fatigued and at times dizzy, so my doctor ordered a hydration drip. Dizziness was also a sign of dehydration.

We had time for Brad to have some lunch before he had to drive me to our first round trip for my treatments. It seemed all so surreal. I was not an easy person to drive with; Due to my two auto accidents and near death experiences, I was overly cautious on the road. I believed some of this came from me being intuitive. I could tell what other cars were going to do before they did it. For example, I could tell if the car next to us was going to quickly change lanes or slam on their brakes. It was more of a curse to have this awareness than a gift.

Even though I was nervous as we made our way down the road, I learned quickly that I enjoyed Brad's way of driving. He was very calm and took his time. He never drove too close to a car, he always used his blinkers, and he was a relaxed, confident driver. I silently thanked God because during his visit I knew we would spend a lot of time driving together.

Hydration was an easy task, but also boring. We sat in the infusion chairs for over an hour as the nurse came in with a bag full of fluids. She hung the bag on the pole and put the drip line into my port where the fluid drained through. The process was painless and easy. All Brad and I had to do now was to relax in our recliners. They offered us snacks and drinks that we could help ourselves to at anytime. It was amazing how I had more energy after the hydration.

Next, Brad drove us to my radiation center. The three radiation technicians and Dr. Steven took the time to meet Brad and show him around. They even took him into the radiation room and described how the machine worked. It was nice for Brad to get to see what I was going through, and for him to ask any questions or concerns that he had to Dr. Steven. When we were leaving, I saw that Brad was pleased to see what a wonderful team I had working with me. On the way home, he shared with me that he felt confident that we were doing all the right treatments.

That evening at home, I explained to my son how well my healing sessions had gone over the past weeks, and how hard I had been working to complete my book. He knew that "Proof of Miracles" meant everything to me. Deep down, I wasn't sure if I was completing this book so others would remember me and my work, if I didn't make it through this. I didn't like to think that way; I knew that it was my humanness and ego getting in the way. My extreme drive I had to complete my book was something that I didn't fully understand. The next morning, I received everything for my book that was needed from my interior book editor and book cover designer. I worked on Amazon, uploading my manuscript and book cover. I was becoming frustrated with the uploading process because every time I clicked to upload my manuscript, Amazon would reject it, saying that the alignment of the interior was incorrect. My margins were off and would not upload properly.

I immediately send the interior designer an email with the subject line reading: "URGENT!" I let her know that Amazon was not accepting the manuscript because the graphic design next to the chapter title was not within the required margins. I told her to please make all the graphic symbols that are placed behind the chapter numbers slightly smaller for all of the chapters to keep the consistency while making them all fall within the margin requirements. Please get this done ASAP so I can upload this before the radio show tomorrow.

2

My Conversation with God Becoming a Healer

This is the corrected image showing the graphic
design next to the chapter title.

Knowing she was most likely sleeping when I sent this email due to her being in another country, all I could do was pray that I would receive this sometime today.

I stepped away from doing this work and into my healing room to do a session. To keep the house quiet during my healing session, Brad decided he would take Layla for a long walk and enjoy the beautiful weather. Back in his hometown, it was snowing and cold. This was a treat for them both.

I was only doing one healing per week now, so I really looked forward to these sessions. Once I stepped into my healing room, I sat in prayer. During this time, I removed my humanness and I let God take over to orchestrate the session. I was able to leave everything that I was dealing with in my own world outside the healing room door. This was a sacred time between my client, myself, and God.

I was always in awe with each of my healing sessions, as each of them were never the same but always so profound. God continued to show me how He used me as His instrument; I felt, saw, heard, and voiced what was going on in my client's body. Whatever was going on in my body no longer affected me. I was able to remove myself from my body and allow God to use it as His instrument, giving me the pain that my clients were dealing with.

This was a gift that God gave me, for when I felt it, I didn't deny what was going on in their body. When the session was over, it was no longer a part of me. Then, I went back to feeling my own health issues. This was amazing and beautiful. God's messages always lifted my Spirit up. He continued to show me I was never alone. I always felt His love surround me and my clients.

At the end of this session, I remained on my healing table for awhile longer. It felt good to relax and stay in the peaceful, loving energy. While my eyes were still closed, I was given a vision: I saw Layla running without her leash, and a sudden panic took over.

I immediately said to God, *please, protect Layla. I don't want her to get hit by a car.* Then, I felt a relief. Not knowing if this was happening or if this was something that was going to happen, I let it go and gave it to God. I didn't want to put anymore energy into it. I continued to relax for a few more minutes until I felt empowered and ready to go back to working on my book.

I decided to move forward and at least get the book cover uploaded to Amazon. Then, everything would be completed and all I would need to do was upload the manuscript when I recieved it.

A message suddenly appeared on my screen from Amazon: "We are sorry. Your book cover cannot be accepted because your pages do not match. Please resubmit and try again."

"Oh my goodness!" I sighed, leaning back in my desk chair in exasperation. I knew this meant that the 6x9 cover size that I had selected the book to be printed in was not matching the cover design of the book I was uploading.

I took a screenshot of the layout that Amazon suggested I use and sent it over by email to my book cover designer. By now, I was in tears.

When Brad returned from his walk with Layla, he saw how this publication nightmare was taking a toll on me emotionally and physically. It was taking every ounce of me to complete this final process, and now with these new difficulties I didn't have it in me to figure this out. I was having a major breakdown when he came to my rescue. He asked me to explain everything that was going on.

My designer emailed me right back, stating he never had any issues before with his designs uploading onto Amazon, and that he was sending the correct format to me. My son and I emailed back and forth with him. He sent us PDF files, but we still had no success. Today was my deadline, and the pressure of getting "Proof of Miracles" live and available for my readers was overwhelming.

"Mom," Brad began after a while, "I think you should walk out of the room and take a deep breath. I'll handle this."

"Are you sure?" I asked.

"Yeah," he said, giving me a reassuring smile. "Trust me. I've worked on programs like this many times for work."

I conceded, and gave him the cell phone number to the designer so they could hopefully figure this problem out over the phone.

Walking into my bedroom, I collapsed on my bed. It was time for me to release this and give it to God. I needed to remove this pressure and let it go. If the book was meant to be finished by tomorrow's radio show, it would, and if not, then it wasn't meant to be. Either way, "Proof of Miracles" was going to be in print, maybe just not in the time that I had worked so hard for it to be completed by.

When talking on the phone, Brad discovered that the format that my designer was sending to us was not correct. What he noticed was that the file was in the wrong size and wrong direction. Brad requested that the designer send him the file through Dropbox, where a larger, correct file could be more easily managed than email.

What they both discovered next was that when the designer sent the correct book cover in a JPG format to my email, the server adjusted the file and sent it in a smaller format. It was the server's fault! I would have never figured this out on my own, and I wasn't sure that my designer would have been able to, either.

Thank God Brad was with me to come to the rescue! He told me to trust him and that he had experience with this, and he proved himself right. I was beyond relieved and ecstatic that this issue was finally resolved.

I was anxious to get the book uploaded to Amazon, knowing this part would be complete, but Brad glanced at the clock and noticed we needed to leave now in order to get to my radiation treatment on time. I had to put the complicated task of my publishing my book down and leave it to do when we returned. Knowing it only took a few minutes to upload, it was hard for me not to do before we left, but I knew I didn't have any more minutes to spare. Leaving, I had hope that my interior manuscript would be sent to me in its final, edited version where I could upload both onto Amazon.

As Brad waited in the waiting room, one of the technicians called my name and brought me back to the radiation room. She watched how I was walking slowly and took a long look into my eyes. As she was checking me in on the computer, she scolded me. She could tell I was not getting enough rest. I was very pale, fragile, and had low energy. All three of the technicians made me very aware of their concerns, too, and how serious it was for me to take the time to rest so my body could heal during these treatments.

They knew I was working hard and spending many hours to get my book finished. I told them that I was close to finishing and should be done in the next two days. They didn't like this answer; they wanted me to put this to rest now.

However, I had an A personality; if I set a goal, I was going to go above and beyond to accomplish that goal, no matter how hard or how much I had to do to complete it.

On the way home, Brad wanted to stop to get a bite to eat at In & Out. It was late now and we both didn't eat anything for lunch because we had worked all morning on the book. We went through the drive-thru, and I decided I would try to eat what I normally ordered: a grilled cheese, with grilled onions.

We ate at the kitchen counter as soon as we got home. I was pleasantly surprised that this was staying in me. "Mom," Brad began as we ate, "I was going to tell you that when I took Layla out for a walk today, she got out of her harness."

I set my sandwich down for a moment and stared at him, remembering the vision I had that morning. "Really?" I asked. "How did that happen?"

"You must not have clicked the leash properly by not putting it on the tighter loops," Brad explained. "She was able to squeeze herself out of it. She kept running towards the cars, so I told Layla, 'if you don't listen to me and you get hit, it's not my fault. Do you really want to die today?'"

"You really said that?" I said, shocked.

"Yeah," Brad replied. "The more I ran towards her, the more she ran. Finally, she noticed that I could outrun her and she gave up. She sat by me and knew she was naughty."

I didn't share with him the vision that I had seen after my healing while he was walking her. I didn't know if he would have believed me. I would have had to share this with him first, then he would have been in awe (not after the fact). I realized that this vision wasn't meant for Brad; it was meant for me. God was showing and validating me with how spot-on and clear I was with my visions and with my work. I was filled with gratitude for this message, and for protecting Layla from getting hit by a car. Thank you, God!

Right after I finished eating, I had to go directly to the couch to lie down. I took my laptop with me, anxious to see if the interior of the book was corrected. I was still determined to get my book cover uploaded onto Amazon. Sadly, I had no emails come in from the interior designer, but I was able to upload the book cover without any issues. Amazon approved it for publication.

That evening as we watched TV, I kept checking my computer hourly in hopes of receiving the final, edited version. Brad let me know he was heading to bed and suggested that I do the same. I decided that I felt really comfortable on the couch and would sleep there.

Unfortunately, I couldn't rest well as my mind would not shut off. I woke up every few hours to check my emails. I had this strength, will, and energy in me to strive to finish my book.

It was 4:00 a.m. when I read the first email from the interior designer saying they were working on correcting the margins. They should have them to me shortly. I scrolled down and there was the second email that said "revised copy ready for print". I quickly downloaded this version onto my desktop, logged into the Amazon page, and uploaded this revised manuscript. Once uploaded, I clicked the button for Amazon's approval. I was shaking and praying at the same time.

Please, God, let this work. I knew mentally I could not handle it if it didn't.

As I waited for a few minutes that seemed to last forever, I closed my eyes and once again gave the control to God. When I opened my eyes, I read: "Amazon has approved the interior design. Click here to approve publication." Oh my goodness! It worked! I clicked the button and the book was now in the publication process with Amazon.

My joy was short-lived, however, when I saw the next notification telling me that it could take up to two weeks for the book to my available for others to purchase. My heart sank. I came this far, but now I had to wait yet again.

I glanced at the clock on my laptop's screen, realizing that the radio show was today at 1:00 p.m., and I moved my radiation treatment later to 3:30. I needed to close my eyes and get a few hours of rest. I felt like a huge weight had been lifted off of my shoulders: I had completed my goal. I finished the book and had it uploaded onto Amazon before the radio show.

"Messages of Hope" with Suzanne Giesemann went extremely well. I felt so much beautiful positive energy flowing through me when I spoke that afternoon. No one would have guessed that I had only a few hours of sleep the night before.

A few friends and colleagues of mine tuned in for the show. They all stated how my story was very uplifting, and how spot-on I was with answering all of the questions Suzanne asked me. I announced for the first time the title of my book, "Proof of Miracles", and that it would be ready to purchase on Amazon any day now. I also said I would post the link to my book for purchase on my website and Facebook page.

The show was a success. I was so grateful to Suzanne for having me as her guest on her show, as it gave me a focus and a goal to reach during a very difficult time in my life. It gave me a purpose and hope to hold onto. By doing so, I was able to give others hope and healing through "Proof of Miracles".

After doing the radio show, my spirit felt uplifted. I loved sharing my story and the message to never lose hope. Now, I had to be the one to not only say those words but to live up to them.

I needed to go get my labs drawn to check my platelet count. Dr. Stephanie was keeping a close watch on me since it dropped to sixty on Monday. On my way to the radiation, Dr. Stephanie called with my results. She said we had good and bad news: The good news was that my platelets had gone up to 67. Bad news was that it was still too low for me to take my chemo pills.

When I arrived for radiation, I was able to let the technicians know I had completed my book and that I would promise to rest the remainder of the day after my sessions. They were happy, and I'm sure they could see the relief in my eyes that I had completed my book and that the radio show was behind me. They knew this meant I would now be able to make more time for me, allowing myself to relax and heal.

After my treatment for the day was complete, Dr. Steven came in to speak with me. He wanted to discuss taking me off of chemo because of my low platelet count.

"I've only been on chemo for thirteen days," I said. "If I stop now, that means I'll miss seventeen more days of treatments. Should I be worried?"

Dr. Steven shook his head. "Actually, Debra," he began matter-of-factly, "I'm not worried about you not having chemo. They haven't always used it with radiation when treating your type of cancer."

"Really?" I asked. My mind relaxed a little when I heard this. "So I don't necessarily need it?"

"When my team and I were planning out your care," Dr. Steven replied, "we felt it would be best to give you all the treatment forms possible, in hopes to get the most effective outcome."

Because of my healing abilities, and my connection with God, I was very in tune with my body, so hearing Dr. Steven say this gave me some peace of mind. After all, I was told by God to see my doctor "now" for a hemorrhoid that I had for thirteen years, and then I was promoted to remove this hemorrhoid even after a doctor told me not to. I trusted the words and the guidance that I received. I couldn't ignore it, and instead chose to honor the words spoken to me and walk through what I was told to do, even if I questioned it.

My body was showing me that it could no longer tolerate the chemo. It had enough and it was done with this form of treatment. I had to thank God for this, as He was guiding me every step of the way. This was all part of His plan for me.

10

———◆———

ALL I WANT IS A BAGEL!

The next day, I woke up to a big surprise: Amazon emailed me saying my paperback book was ready for purchase! I had to blink and re-read the message to be sure. Was I really reading this correctly? They said the usual turn-around time from download to print was within two weeks. This had only taken one day! At that moment, I knew God had His hands on "Proof of Miracles". Only God could have made this happen. He once again worked behind the scenes.

I was so pleased that my book cover designer created a Facebook header page with the cover of my book. I uploaded this onto my Facebook page and proudly made my book release announcement:

"Abundant Blessings To All!

"My new book, 'Proof of Miracles' by Debra Martin is now available on Amazon. May the profound healing testimonies in this book remind you how much you are loved and always surrounded by Grace. Using the tools at the beginning of each chapter, my hope is that you come to this conclusion: 'My miracle is but a breath away!'

"Click on the link below to order your copy today!"

Once I posted this, it was another huge weight off my shoulders, and another goal accomplished. The people that were listening to the radio show and even others now would know where to purchase my book. After my radiation treatment, Brad asked if there was anything that I wanted to get for lunch. He was going to stop and get Mexican food on our way home, but I asked if he would please make an extra stop on the way to pick up In and Out for me. My grilled cheese with grilled onions stayed down the first time, so I felt it would be safe to try this again.

I decided to eat mine in the car, as it was going to be awhile before we got home since we still had to stop for his food. After he paid and reached for his order through the carry out window, my stomach suddenly began to cramp. Oh no! I was in trouble. This time, this food wasn't sitting well with me. I pleaded for Brad to please get home as fast as he could.

There was no rhyme or reason to what food I was going to react or not react to. This made it frustrating and stressful to eat anything. Not knowing if I was going to be okay, the anxiety that came from this made me feel safer not eating. I thought it would be better to go back to eating little amounts at a time. This seemed to work the best. My radiation from that day had to trigger this area.

Later that day, my neighbor Larry offered to cook salmon for all of us for dinner. So that I would not have to smell any of the food getting cooked, he said he would like to come down and visit for awhile first. He arrived with a lovely bottle of cabernet in his hand. The three of us went out on the back patio to enjoy the weather, and Brad and Larry opened the bottle of wine.

I was somewhat jealous, as I would have loved to relax and enjoy a glass with the both of them. Brad even commented a few times on how good the wine was. About an hour or so later, Larry invited Brad over to his house to show him his technique on preparing his marinade and grilling the salmon. It was nice seeing the two of them having a wonderful time together.

Larry knew that I loved the way he cooked his salmon. I know he made this in hopes that I would eat more. They returned not long after with the salmon and asparagus. We all sat at my round table in my kitchen. Brad was loving the salmon and explaining on how he liked to make his version, but I struggled to eat and wanted to show my appreciation by eating more than a couple of bites.

I finished two tiny pieces that were the size of a quarter. Both Larry and Brad tried to have me take seconds, but I could barely keep what I ate down. This was the most I had eaten in a long time. I was very tired, but I wanted to stay at the table with them to enjoy their conversations.

Within ten minutes after I ate, I ran to the bathroom and everything came back out. *How can so much come out when I ate so little?* I was contemplating going to lay down in my bed, but knew I needed to be in the other room with them, so I retired on the couch.

After dinner, they joined me on the couch and had another glass of wine. Larry went back down to two doors to his house to grab them some dessert. They both enjoyed a brownie covered with hot fudge, ice cream, and two girl scout cookies.

Feeling a little better, I looked at my son. "Do you think I could have a bite of your brownie?"

He stared at me, and the look on his face said, "how dare you ask? This is all mine!"

"Really," I said with a smile, "how much can I eat?"

He handed me his fork and I tried one tiny bite. It was very tasty, but a little too rich for my tummy. Brad was in Heaven!

Larry could tell that I wasn't doing very well. I had to stay lying down and was not adding much to the conversation. My abdomen was in pain and I could hardly keep my eyes open. I had to excuse myself a few times to run to the bathroom. It was very embarrassing.

After the third time, I thanked Larry for cooking a wonderful dinner and evening, but I let him know that I had to retire to my bed. He understood. We gave hugs and shortly after I left the room, he went home. It was very kind of Larry to spend this evening with us. He brought some joy into the house, which helped my brain to refocus and stopped me from thinking about how miserable I was feeling.

I was still in bed when I heard my phone ringing the next morning. Allison was calling to let me know she was going to the minute clinic to be examined to see if she was contagious. She was doing her part to make sure she wouldn't get me sick. As bad as I felt knowing she was doing this, it also gave me a sense of relief. I didn't have to be the bad guy anymore.

"I did have a cold, Mom," she told me, "but I fought it off and now it's just allergies I'm dealing with. So it's safe for me to come home!"

"That's great, honey!" I told her, sitting up in bed and petting Layla next to me.

"I can be home later this afternoon," Allison said, her voice gleeful on the other end. I knew she was happy because she'd have a chance to see her brother before he had to go home.

I was feeling that my body really needed some substance to help control my diarrhea. I wanted to add a few carbs back into my body, but I knew I'd need to convince both of my sons that this was the plan I felt my body now needed. In the back of my mind, all I heard was "carbs feed cancer cells." These words haunted me, but I needed a change in my diet. This was no longer working.

Both Steven and Brad were very stern when it came to me following my doctor's order of not eating any carbs. I knew when I mentioned that I wanted to introduce a few carbs now before my treatment was over, they were not going to support this. I knew they meant well as they wanted the best for me. They felt if I followed this diet, I would be helping kill my cancer. What they didn't understand was that I knew my body better than them, and even better than the doctors. I had to trust that the change I wanted was okay for me, as I knew it was going to help me get through my treatments.

Brad was still in his bedroom when he received my text. I thought hard as I composed the message, trying to write the correct words for him to accept my wishes. I was really craving a bagel, so I texted: "how about we have an egg (good protein), with avocado (good fats) on a toasted bagel for breakfast?" I saved the bagel for last, feeling this was a good compromise. I was still eating healthy.

Not much later in the morning, Brad and I stood in the kitchen. "So your breakfast choice sounds great, Mom," he began, ". . . minus the bagel."

I should have known better, but I couldn't take it. I let out a sob and plopped onto the sofa, tears streaming down my face.

"I'll make you scrambled eggs with a banana on the side, okay?" Brad tried now. "Let's start with that."

There were too many emotions running through me, however, and all I could think was that if I didn't have something more solid, breakfast was going to go right through me. I cried like a child throwing a tantrum. "I don't like scrambled eggs!" I said. "They don't sound appealing to me. Can you please just go to the store and buy me a bagel?"

"Let me cook this first," Brad insisted, taking the eggs out of the fridge. "Let's just see if you can keep this down."

Before he started cooking, Brad called his older brother Steven and placed him on speaker. He explained how I wanted to eat a bagel, and that's when I knew I'd hear the same thing all over again.

"Mom," came Steven's voice from Brad's phone. "You know carbs are not good for you. Why are you willing to put them in your body? We need to stay strong and eat the right foods to fight this the right way."

This only made me bawl harder. They didn't understand how my stomach cramped every time I ate. The pain I was going through and the emotional stress of hoping I would make it to the bathroom on time were too much to handle. I was beginning to not want to eat at all, as the consequences were not very pleasant.

"It's pretty difficult to feed her," Brad was saying to Steven. "She barely eats anything and nothing ever sounds good to her. Be prepared for what you're in for when you come see her. It's not easy to do or to watch her go through."

I was trying to be a good patient, but I could not handle the smells of food and the thought of eating sounded horrific. I tried to explain the side effects from the chemo pill, Xeloda, but neither of my sons would hear me out. They felt they were following my doctor's directions and knew what was best for *my* body.

As Brad cooked the eggs, the smell made me very nauseous. When he brought over the plate, the look of the eggs made me squeamish. "I don't think I can do this," I murmured, putting a hand up to my mouth.

"Please," Brad insisted. "Do this for me."

It took everything I had in me to put the fork close to my mouth, let alone place the eggs in my mouth. I could barely chew them without gagging. I ate a quarter of the scrambled eggs that were on the plate.

"Try to eat more, Mom," Brad said, and I took another couple of bites of eggs and a few bits of the banana.

"Brad," I began, finally putting my "Mom voice" on and looking him straight in the eye. "Please get this plate out of my sight or I may throw up on it."

I was emotionally exhausted and needed to nap, but only a few minutes after I ate I was running to the bathroom. I felt depleted once again. When I returned to the couch, I could tell that Brad knew from the look in my eyes that I was not feeling well and that the food did not stay down.

Infuriated that I could not eat what I felt my body needed, I grabbed my computer and logged into the healthcare center website. I sent a message to Dr. Stephanie. I would be seeing her on Monday after my labs, and I wanted to discuss my dietary plan with her. I also let her know about the battle that I was having against my children.

I was determined for Brad and Steven to see that reintroducing some carbs was okay. I had shared with them that I remembered the doctors saying that there would come a time when I wouldn't want to eat, and when that happened, I should eat anything that sounded good to me. Unfortunately, they didn't believe me because they didn't hear it from the doctors themselves.

Well, now on Monday Brad could hear it for himself.

After sending off this message, I took a deep breath to collect myself. I didn't want this disagreement to be the focus for the remainder of the weekend. I decided that I would not eat carbs to keep everyone happy. I wanted to enjoy the time with Brad, and Allison, who would be home in a few hours.

Later that day they went out grocery shopping and running a few errands. One of the errands was to purchase a dog grooming electric razor. The two of them came up with the clever idea that they could cut Layla's hair. I offered for her to go to the groomers but they were trying to save me money. I thought this was very kind and would be something fun that the two of them could do together.

I was surprised at how much my son was taking interest in Layla. When we saw him at Thanksgiving he didn't really pay much attention to her at all. It didn't seem like he wanted anything to do with her. So to see him connect the way he was here was very unexpected. The way they bonded together I would have never imagined would happen in a million years.

He took Layla on hour walks in the park, playing with her constantly and even taught her how to not lick his face (kiss), but instead how to hug him. Layla hugged him in a way that she didn't do for anyone else. He picked her up and she immediately snuggled her face on the side of his cheek. It was the cutest thing to watch. Layla had traded us in for him.

She was now sleeping with him, waiting at every door for him to come through, and didn't want anything to do with us if he was around. She even listened and obeyed him better than she did with us. I thought, *what the heck is going on?* But it was a nice break for me. I was able to get some rest without her trying to get my attention. One trick that he did that we all thought was comical was when she would get over-active, he would hold her in both of his hands over his head. When he did this, she became totally still and it calmed her down to where even her heart rate would immediate slow down. Allison and I now do this when we feel she is too overwound.

Brad brought the work out weights in the living room so that he could keep me company while he worked out. His thoughtfulness helped calm my nerves. We watched a few movies together and hung out on the couch outside on the patio and inside in the living room. We spent the day sharing stories of his childhood, our family, and how he was enjoying his life now. It was a wonderful day, filled with many good memories and lots of love.

11

LET GO AND LET GOD

Allison was up early, getting ready for school and out the door by 6:30 a.m. She yelled over her shoulder, "Bye, Mom! I love you!" This was our normal routine, and I was glad that she was home as I replied, "Love you, too! Have a wonderful day."

Today I needed to get my labs drawn again to see where my platelets count was. Dr. Stephanie was hoping that I would get my last big push of Mitomycin-C on Thursday, just a few days from now.

After my labs, I went upstairs to meet with Dr. Stephanie. The nurse took us back where she took my weight and blood pressure. "Are you nervous, Debra?" she asked. "Your blood pressure is higher than normal."

"No, I told her, "but I find it takes a lot of energy for me to walk even small distances. That's probably why my blood pressure is up."

Brad sat in the chair next to me and when my doctor entered, she sat on a high stool directly across from us. She asked me how I was feeling, how I was handling my food intake, and if I still was experiencing any diarrhea.

"To be honest," I began, "I always feel depleted and weak. The diarrhea has not stopped. And. . .we are struggling over an issue at home with what I should or shouldn't be eating. I know I was told not to eat any carbs, but now I feel that my body needs more substance to help with my bathroom issues. My family is fighting me on this. I know they want what is best for me, but I feel my body needs this."

By the time I finished voicing my thoughts, I was crying. I was so overwhelmed with emotion over this issue that I had caused myself a lot of stress.

"Well, Debra," began my doctor, "it was Dr. Steven who advised you to do a no carb diet. There are no hard facts that this does help or not help someone who is taking treatments. At this point in your treatment, and with what is going on with your body, we want you to be getting the most nutrition that you can right now. Therefore, we don't care what you eat. We want you to eat anything that you desire or that you can tolerate. If that's a bagel, then you go ahead and eat it."

I was surprised that she referenced the bagel from the email I sent her. It made me happy to know she read my email and was prepared to speak about it during our visit.

"Do you have any other concerns?" she asked now.

"I'm a little worried about her mental status," Brad spoke up. "Should she be put on any antidepressants to help her with any anxiety or depression."

I held my breath and bit my tongue. *Is he really asking about that for me?* I thought, taken aback. *But. . . he is doing it out of love.* I waited to hear her response.

"I can't prescribe Debra any pills for anxiety or depression," she said, looking at Brad. "I do feel that if this is coming from her treatments, it will all go away after she is finished." She paused, then made eye contact with me. "Debra, if you feel this is something that you need, then you would need to seek help from your primary doctor."

I glanced at my son for a moment, thinking of what to say next. I was always very honest, and knew that, no matter what was put in my way, I would never lose hope. "I do feel anxiety at times," I confessed, "and depression does set in when I have no control of my bowels. This does take a toll on me; however, I feel these emotions are real for what I am going through. I don't feel I need or want any pills to help me with this matter. In my mind, I know that it's important to recognize these feelings. Emotions are energy, and I need to feel them and acknowledge them. I will walk through everything I feel and place my emotions in my prayers each step of the way. I can surrender and release them as they come."

The doctor passed me more tissues, as I was crying even more now. "Good," she said with a smile. "Now, today's platlet count came in at 74. I'm pleased to see that it went up, but we can't do the last push on Thursday unless your count is 100 or above. It could be life-threatening. Can you come by on Thursday in the morning to draw blood, then see if we can move toward in the afternoon?"

I looked at my son and nodded. That would work with our schedule, if I came here first, then went to the radiation treatment, then made it back here to the infusion chair.

"Great," my doctor said. "In the meantime, I think it would be a good idea if you came in for another hydration treatment tomorrow."

I thought this was a great idea, and so did Brad. He had seen how much better I felt after the last one, and we made an appointment with the nurse before we left.

We all stood up and my doctor came over and gave me a big hug. "You are handling things so well with such grace," she said softly. "I'm proud of you. Go and get some rest."

I returned her embrace, knowing that she meant I wasn't just her patient; I mattered. She was looking out for what was best for me. I felt her genuine compassion and love.

As we left the office and made our way back to the car, I said, "Are you going to tell your siblings that the doctor said I could add carbs to my diet now?"

"No," Brad replied. "I'm sorry, I just don't fully agree with your doctor."

"I'll do my best to limit the amount of carbs," I told him, trying my best to compromise so he would be happy, too. His expression softened a little then, and I felt that by me saying this, he would feel better about our next steps moving forward.

We couldn't get to the radiation center fast enough. I was starting to sweat and was praying: *please, God. . . let me make it to the bathroom on time!* As soon as we pulled up to the curb, I got out of the car and ran as fast as I could to the bathroom, praying again that it was available. Whew! I barely made it. Everything was exploding out of me. *How could I possibly go this much?* Once I was finished, all of my anxiety went away. I was able to sit in the waiting room without worry. I was confident that I would be fine until we got home.

Strangely, I had started to enjoy going to radiation. It wasn't the radiation that I looked forward to, but seeing the three nurses. We had created a special bond, often sharing what they did over the weekend with their kids, where they traveled, hiked, etc. These nurses had compassion like I had never witnessed before. If they ever said, "Debra, you look tired", I would begin to cry, knowing that they really understood me.

There were times that I would cry and they immediately comforted me. "Don't cry," they said, "or we'll all start crying!" There were times when we all did. The way they walked and guided me into and out of the room, to the way they helped position my body correctly on the radiation table, to placing my white blanket on me each day to keep me warm made me feel so loved.

"Okay, ladies," I said to them as they left the room so the treatment could begin. "This is my quiet time when I get to pray and close my eyes. My nap time. My God time."

That evening, I had a small piece of plain french bread with a few bits of chicken. Oh my gosh! Not only did it taste good, it *felt* good eating it. I savored every bite.

In bed that night, I felt really nervous about getting my last push. I dreaded thinking about having to go through all of the agony of this treatment all over again. That's when I felt a strong knowing set within me. My heart began to race, and I felt that if I had this last push of Mitomycin-C, I may not survive. My heart would not be able to take it.

All I could do was to pray and put this challenge into God's hands. He would know what was best for me.

Please, God, I prayed in the darkness of my room. *If this medicine is going to be more harmful than helpful. . . don't let my platelets go up high enough tomorrow.*

Tuesday was Brad's last day. I had some boxes of his that he wanted to go through, so he did this in the family room so that I could be a part of his decision making. He chose what he still wanted, what he could take home with him now, which items he no longer wanted that we would donate, and which items he would save for taking home at another visit. Each item was a conversational piece, which made this lots of fun.

We had to add my hydration treatment at 1:00 p.m. into our schedule, followed by my radiation treatment at 2:30. Brad finished going through all of the boxes, but he didn't have time to pack them. He decided to do this later when we returned.

I found it interesting that I had a hydration treatment on the day Brad arrived and again on his last day. Hydration was easy and re-laxing. We found a private room in the back were we both sat back and chatted about both our upcoming week's schedules. A few of the nurses that I had gotten to know from my first push came in to say hi. They also said they thought I was doing very well, considering the amount of radiation I had endured. On my first push day, I had wondered how I would feel when I reached week five, and if I would be able to sit or if I would have to lay down for my last treatment. I was very grateful that I was able to sit in the hydration chair without any pain or issues. The nurses each gave me a hug and said they would see me on Thursday for my last push.

I didn't say anything, because as nice as it would be to see them, I was hoping that these hugs would be the last time. I was still holding onto the fact that I may not have to go through with the last push. The hour was up and my next stop was radiation.

Radiation went quickly and before long we were back in the car driving home. I thanked Brad for being a cautious and calm driver. He laughed and said, "That's good to hear, Mom. My girlfriend thinks that I drive way too slow, like an old person." We both laughed.

I didn't eat much for dinner that night, as I was feeling really weak and having abdominal pain. I was also felt really cold. This was still side effects of my chemo; bringing my body temperature lower. It seemed like I could never get warm, on top of being extremely tired all the time. Occasionally, I woke up during the night with my bones aching throughout my body. I tried to rub this pain out of my legs and arms as best as I could. The fatigue was really setting in from my radiation treatments.

Being off chemo helped me feel fairly well during the time Brad was visiting. I wasn't getting the diarrhea like I had when I was taking the chemo pills. We had a few nights when my temperature rose to 102, which was too high for a chemo patient. My doctors do not want it to go over 100.4F, and if it did they said we had to contact them immediately, day or night. With the doctors' guidance, we were always able to control my temperature with Tylenol.

I noticed my temperature spiked in the early evenings after my radiation treatments. I believed it was a sign showing me that my body was under a lot of stress and needed even more rest. Dr. Stephanie did run a blood test to see if I had any infections going on, but they came back negative. I saw how the treatments were starting to kick in and were getting the best of me.

After Allison went to bed, Brad and I had time to talk alone before he would get picked up for the airport at 11:00 p.m. "Thank you, honey," I said sincerely. "For everything you've done for me. I couldn't have survived this far without you."

Brad smiled. "Was I a good caretaker?"

"You did an outstanding job!" I said. "You made everything seem effortless, and you brought joy back into my house. You took the pressure off your little sister by helping with dinner and getting groceries with her. And," I added with a grin, "Layla is *really* going to miss you! If anything ever happens to me, Layla is your dog."

He actually laughed at that. "Well, I'll be back to see you again soon. I don't think I have as much patience as you say, so I'd like to be here on the easiest week your doctors said you'll need someone."

After what I'd witnessed now, I thought Brad would have been able to handle any of my treatment weeks just fine, but I nodded anyway. "I've been blessed to have time with you alone. I'll miss you when you're gone."

I was able to see another side of Brad that was so loving, open, and kind that I didn't get to see when we gathered with the entire family. I understood why he put his walls up, as he was preparing for what may or may not happen when we were all together. When my children got together, there always seemed to be a controversial conversation that arose that often turned hurtful or argumental.

"You know," I said to Brad, taking his hand, "it would be nice if your other siblings could get to know this other side of you."

My hope was that with the time I spent alone with each of my children, I would help them see how valuable and short life was. Things could change in a split second. They couldn't take life for granted, and they should live life to the fullest. Most importantly, I wanted them to see how we as a family had each other's backs, and that we were there for one another. They should always remember the love we shared as a family; it was a strong, unbreakable, and unconditional bond.

When it was time for Brad to leave, reality really hit me hard. I hugged him extra-long and embraced him, firmly hoping he would never forget this hug that was filled with love. I truly didn't know if this would be the last time that we would spend quality alone time together. There were still a lot of unknowns ahead.

This time that God was giving me was a gift of time with my children. Was this because my life was coming to an end, or was it Him showing me how much my children truly loved me? I always knew my children loved me, but I have never seen this type of worry, care, and outpouring compassion.

They showed me that they would do anything at any given time, giving me anything and all that I needed to make sure that their mom was okay. The depths of this went beyond what I could explain. I knew for certain that I was one lucky mom! God blessed me with four children who were beautiful on the inside and out.

When I heard the door close behind Brad, I fell apart. His flight out was at 1:00 a.m and Steven's flight would arrive at 9:00 a.m. My children planned this well. I would have Allison with me throughout the night, and would only be alone for a few hours in the morning before Steven would arrive.

When my oldest son walked in the house with his work bag and luggage, he found me resting on the couch. I was up early which gave me the time to shower, do my healing session, and try to pull myself together so that I would look somewhat normal. I wanted his first impression of me to be good and not terrifying.

A few years ago, Steven lost his best friend to cancer and witnessed how the disease had destroyed him. This was hard for my son to witness and to face. His friend made such an impact on his life that he named his daughter's middle name after him. I was trying to show him that what I was going through was different.

"Wow, Mom!" Steven exclaimed. "You look good. I was expecting to see you so much worse."

I wondered if this was good or bad. I may have been looking good on the outside, but I was feeling lousy on the inside. My health had turned for the worst. I was feeling the effects from the cumulative treatments now. My body and God were telling me that I needed some time off to heal. I knew I needed to cancel the two sessions that were scheduled for the first two weeks of April.

I reached out to Valerie to let her know what was happening. I felt bad that I was unable to help those that she had already scheduled, but Valerie was proud of me for listening to my body. This was a lesson for me to put myself first. I needed to honor my body and give myself permission to take this time to heal. In doing so, I hoped I would heal quicker and return to work sooner.

I updated my calendar to show that I would begin sessions again on April 17th. Then, I would take it slow I only do one healing per week through the first two weeks of May. That meant I would have one month of doing one session per week. I felt this was a goal that I could accomplish.

Today, Steven only had to drive me for my radiation treatment. I was getting very nervous about the infusion that I would receive tomorrow, if my platelets went above 100 or more. I wanted Steven to understand why I wasn't wanting this next push, but wasn't sure how I was going to present this to him without him getting upset. I decided that would be a discussion that I would save for later.

He wanted to take the freeway to get to my appointment quicker, but I let him know that we couldn't because this gave me anxiety. He didn't question my words and honored my request. I noticed that his brain was always working, and he constantly had to check his phone at every stop light. His driving didn't worry me, but his inability to rest his mind did.

By the time we returned home, Allison was back from school. They decided they wanted to order pizza for our dinner. Steven understood that I could now eat carbs, but that I was limiting them. When the pizza arrived, I took one look at it and knew I shouldn't eat it. I commented on how much grease the pizza had, but it didn't bother either of them; Steven and Allison dug right in and enjoy every bite. I decided I would slice a few pieces of cheese, and that was enough to satisfy me. I didn't have much of an appetite nowadays.

After Steven finished getting his things arranged in his room, he came and sat with me on the couch. I decided it was a good time to bring up what tomorrow's push day was going to look like.

As I thought over the timing of each appointment tomorrow, I started to cry. I was full of emotions, and the thought of getting the infusion was really weighing on me. "Steven," I began, wiping off my wet cheeks, "I have to tell you that I really hope my count isn't high enough. I don't feel like this infusion is good for my body." I sat up and made sure I looked straight into my son's eyes. "In fact, I feel it may be more harmful than good. I have a strong feeling that it would be too much for my body to handle. My heart won't be able to take it."

Steven gave me an unsure look, and I could tell that he wasn't going to be on my side. He and the rest of my family all felt the same way: I needed to go through this last push to make sure I killed all of the cancer. "Mom," he replied, "you've come this far; you can't quit now. You really should do this, then you won't ever have to do it again."

I sighed, knowing there wasn't anything else I could say to change this mind. "Well," I said, "we'll just have to wait and see what my labs reveal."

What my family had a hard time understanding was that I knew my body very well. As a healer, God showed me and let me know with visions what would happen if I got this infusion. If my vision was real, then I had to trust that God was in control. He would make sure my platelets were not high enough to have this infusion. I had to trust that He knew if this was going to cause me more harm than good. He would do what was best for me.

I also had to trust my body. It was guiding me all along this journey with my work. If my platelets showed up low, then my body was saying enough is enough. I had received all the chemo that my body needed, and that all the cancer would be gone. I would be healed.

Because everyone in my house felt indifferent, we all went to bed a little unsettled that night. None of us liked to make each other feel bad, but we each had the right to feel the way we did.

12

WALKING WITH GRATITUDE

From Day One, I wondered how I was going to feel on Day 28. It had always seemed so far away. Each day, I looked at the calendar and counted the days until my next infusion. I knew that, once I reached this day, I only had nine more days left.

I remember the first infusion push day, sitting in the infusion chair and looking at those that were extremely ill in the other rooms. I was so worried wondering if I was going to be able to sit or have to lay down on one of those beds later on. What would my pain level would be from all of my radiation treatments? Would my butt be so sore and inflamed that it would be hard to walk, sit, or even get comfortable?

That morning, I was so grateful that so far I could still sit and still walk normally. I could choose whether to sit in one of those rooms or not. I did sit in there once when I had a hydration treatment when all of the other chairs were taken outside of the rooms. It was nice to have a quiet space removed from others. As I got ready to go, I decided I would be at peace with wherever today led us.

We made it on time getting my blood drawn and to my radiation treatment at 11:00 a.m. The radiation nurses could see my worry, as it must have been written all over my face. They took one look at me and asked me what was wrong.

"Today is my last infusion day," I shared. "That is. . . if I can get it."

They both gave me bright smiles and positive words of encouragement. It gave me strength, knowing I was in good hands either way. During my radiation treatment, I tried to rest my mind and relax. Unfortunately, once I settled down, the treatment was over.

As Steven and I got into the car, my phone rang. It was Dr. Stephanie calling with the results. My heart dropped into my stomach, and I had to take a deep breath before answering. "Hi, Dr. Stephanie." I placed her on speaker phone so Steven could hear, too.

"Good morning, Debra," came my doctor's voice. "So, your platelets have only come up two points from 74 to 76. At this point, having this infusion would be more harmful to your body. As I've said before, it's standard protocol to not proceed unless our count is 100 or higher."

"Well, what happens if she doesn't get this infusion?" Steven asked, his strong voice very concerned. "Will my mom not be getting all of the treatment she needs to fight this cancer?"

"No, she will be fine," Dr. Stephanie replied. "She's received all that we can give her."

I could tell from the hard expression on Steven's face that he wasn't happy with this answer. "Then why would we even consider giving her another dose of this medicine when we know how harsh it was on her body the first time?"

"This is an old protocol that we follow," my doctor responded. "We've seen lots of success with the second infusion. But, many of my patients have not be able to take the second infusion and were fine in the end."

Steven, however, still wasn't satisfied. "So we are following old protocols when we know they may or may not work?" he questioned.

"Like I said, we have seen lots of success with this protocol of doing the second infusion," Dr. Stephanie clarified. "But your mother will be fine if she doesn't do another infusion today. We don't want her to have an infusion that could bring her platelet counts even lower. Then, she could need a platelet infusion or be more at risk for infection or bleeding. This would be more harmful to her than beneficial."

Steven asked one more question: "Can she have this infusion when her platelets go back up before the end of her treatments on the 10th of April?"

"We have to follow the protocol of only giving this infusion on the 1st and the 28th day of treatment."

Steven said, "okay", and then I stepped in and thanked Dr. Stephanie for her call. I wanted to make sure she knew that if we sounded stern it was only because we were concerned. After ending the call, I could tell that Steven wasn't too happy, but I was. I was so relieved that there were tears brimming in my eyes. I felt like I could breathe. The heaviness that I was holding onto in my chest was finally removed. God was good! The premonition He showed me was that this was going to be more harmful than helpful, and that is what we were told today. Wow!

Now, I knew my family had to trust that I was going to be okay with the treatments that I had, and with the ones I would continue to receive.

The rest of the day went well. We ordered food again for dinner. This time they wanted Mexican, and I decided I would try to have a tostada, thinking this would probably be my most healthy and safe choice. We enjoyed sitting on the back patio, chatting and enjoying our meal. I was pleasantly surprised that my food stayed down. I didn't have any issues with it. I was so happy to be able to eat something without cramping or it coming right out of me.

In the early evening, Allison decided to take Steven to the ice cream shop in town where their ice cream was homemade each day. It was nice to see the two of them doing something together without me, and doing something fun that would get them out of the house for a little bit.

That night when I went to bed, I had a lot to be grateful for. I needed to take the time to sit in prayer, thanking God for everything He did for me. I knew that He was working behind the scenes, and knowing that He was aware of every step before I took it brought me great comfort. I slept at ease that night knowing that I only had nine more radiation treatments to go. My sister would be arriving at the end of the month.

I hoped she was okay with coming out early. She had planned on being here with Steven after my second infusion, thinking it might take both of them to help me. They would have each other to lean on if things got tough. We still didn't know what was ahead for me. Dr. Steven had estimated that the last few weeks of radiation and a few weeks after, I would feel my worst from the side effects. I trusted that all was in order just as it was meant to be.

Steven worked all morning from my home, and we were ready to leave in the afternoon for radiation. I was extremely exhausted, so I rested on the couch until it was time to leave. I guessed that I was feeling the effects from all of the emotions that I went through the previous day.

After radiation, Steven wanted to stop by a comic book store. He said it was a new hobby of his. It helped take his mind off of work when he focused on the stories. He found them fascinating and was getting his three year old daughter to like them, too. The store was close to the radiation center, so it made sense for us to go together. I decided to wait in the car as he ventured inside, so I he could take his time I could make a phone call to my dear friend Jan, who lived in New York and relax.

I spent a good amount of time talking with Jan while Steven was comic book shopping. At times, it got hot in the car and I had to open my door. Steven took the keys, so I couldn't put the air on. It was about an hour later when he walked out of the store with a big grin on his face. He told me all about the comics, the owner of the store, and everything he had learned. That hour wait was well worth the happiness that he received. Plus, I was thrilled that I could sit that long without having to run to the bathroom.

It was now getting late, and Steven was really hungry. He didn't eat much before we left and asked if we could go grab a bite to eat. I had not gone out to eat with Brad when he was visiting, and I really wasn't ready to go out that day. I hadn't planned it mentally, and physically I looked like a wreck. Steven told me I should be proud of who I was, and should be able to go into any place without makeup, not doing my hair, or caring if I was not dressed up enough. This was going to be a huge challenge for me. I didn't want to be around people, so we had to sit on a patio. I didn't want to stay long, as I may have to run to the bathroom and wanted to do that at home.

We went to a place close to home. Steven ordered his dinner and I ordered sweet potatoes and BBQ chicken. I wasn't able to eat them all, so I gave the rest to him to finish. I could feel my tummy rumbling, and I started to panic. I wanted to get home as soon as possible.

"Steven," I began, "let's get the bill. And please let them know we are in a hurry!"

It took forever to get his credit card back, and after a while Steven realized that it was on the table. *Oh my goodness,* I thought, exasperated. *Really?* I was losing my patience, as I was frantically panicking, hoping I would not only make it out to the restaurant, but also into the car and home without having an accident.

I made it home, but just in time. Everything that I had eaten was now coming out. My body was not ready for that type of food. With the anxiety I got not having control of my bowels, I wanted to always stay home. This literally took everything out of me and physically drained me. I was out of commission for the rest of the night. Steven was exhausted, too. He fell asleep faster than I did on the couch. We slept there until Allison woke us up to go to bed.

The next day was beautiful, and Steven, Allison, and I were re-laxing outside on the patio. They both were craving Mexican food again. "Mom," they insisted, "it was okay the first time you had it. You should give it a try again. Plus, beans are good for you; they will give you some protein."

Allison ran to pick it up, and by the time she returned, Steven was asleep on the couch. I had noticed how tired he was. Was it because it was hard for him to see me this way? Or was he tired from working long hours and having two young children to come home to? Maybe it was a combination of both.

Allison and I decided to go out in the backyard and eat on the pa-tio. I again ordered a tostada, bean and cheese only. This time it didn't sit too well; within ten minutes after I finished eating, I was running to the bathroom. I barely made it. I felt so depleted. I couldn't even enjoy something as simple as this with my daughter.

It changed both of our moods. Allsion felt bad for me and said, "at least you tried, Mom." All I wanted to do was cry and go into my bedroom, but I know this would only make her feel worse, so I re-frained and went to the couch. My abdomen was still cramping, and this had once again exhausted me. I had to close my eyes and try to sleep to give my body some rest. I snuggled into the opposite side of the couch along with Steven.

Allison was disappointed that Steven didn't eat the food she bought for him. When she left to pick up our lunch, he went to the couch in the living room and then slept for most of the afternoon. I could see that he was very exhausted. He had been sleeping a lot, and even mentioned that it felt so good to sleep but that he was sorry.

"There's no reason to be sorry," I told him. "It's nice to have someone to rest with me." I was glad to see that he was getting a break from his normal daily routines, and that he was also benefiting from being here.

Allison had to be at work by 4:00 p.m, and Steven decided he would meet up with his step dad to watch the game and grab a bite for dinner.

I was excited that no one would be home so that I could make myself a baked potato for dinner. My body was craving a carb, and I knew it was going to help me balance out my digestive issues. It seemed like it took forever to cook in the oven. As I sliced open the baked potato, the aroma of the steam didn't bother me. I decided that it would be best if I ate it plain; no butter and no seasonings.

I sat on the couch and slowly began to enjoy my wonderful potato. I'd never had a potato that tasted so good. It took me almost an hour to finish eating it, but I was so proud of myself that I ate both halves that I took a picture and sent in on our family group texts. I didn't get the reaction that I was hoping for. They were not happy that I indulged in eating so many carbs.

Steven came home later than I had expected, which annoyed me. There was no reason for me to be annoyed, other than my own selfish emotions that he was able to go out and that I had been stuck inside the house for weeks. I wanted my normal life back of going out with friends and enjoying a bite to eat. I missed laughing and living life. It seemed like life had stopped. Steven could tell that I was annoyed, and I felt bad later that I didn't embrace him with love when he returned. He did nothing wrong and I made him feel bad that he didn't come home earlier or stay in with me.

I had to go back to the attitude of gratitude, being grateful that my son had come out to take care of me.

I was excited that my sister Cindy was arriving the next afternoon. That gave me plenty of time to relax, take my time to shower, and pull myself together. Nowadays, it took a lot of my energy to get ready, and sometimes I just couldn't do it. That day, I had to settle for wearing a baseball cap and no makeup.

My friend Amy gave me a blue army hat as a gift. It was being well used, especially on the days that I only had to get my radiation treatments. It also made me feel not so bad that I couldn't wash my hair, as this cap gave me a lot of strength. When I wore this army hat, it reminded me that my army was with me. I felt as if they were holding me up and giving me the strength to walk.

I was noticing that it was taking a lot of energy to walk from my bedroom to my living room, which wasn't that far. I was out of breath by the time I reached the couch. My body was very weak as it fought the beast inside of me. I had to try and stay positive and not allow my bowel issues to get me depressed. I knew having Cindy with me would be good for us all. She would uplift all of our spirits, and we needed it after the hard week.

I was relaxing on the couch with Steven when Cindy arrived. Allison ran to the door to greet her. Hearing her voice as she walked through the door made me smile. As soon as she saw me, she said the same as Steven: "Wow, Deb! You look great. I was thinking I would see you looking much worse." I told her that right now I was feeling pretty well compared to the last few weeks.

"If I would have had my infusion, you would have been seeing a completely different person," I explained. "I am glad that you both don't have to see me that way. It was so awful. I don't wish anyone to have to experience what I went through."

As Cindy bent down to give me a hug, I immediately started to cry. "I'm really glad that you're here," I whispered. "I need my big sister." Then she began to cry. We were both a slobbering mess.

As she sat on the couch next to me, she told us it has been hard on her not coming out weeks earlier. She felt helpless, as she wasn't able to really see how I was doing, and what truly was going on behind the scenes. She wanted to help me during these difficult times. It was hard when family lived far away, especially when someone was in need of help.

Cindy and I had a wonderful relationship. We shared everything with one another. It was really special to have a sister who I also considered my best friend. Even though we lived far from one another, she had always been there for me through the good times and bad. I was blessed to have her as my sister. She was an angel on earth. She was the type of person who put everyone first, never said no, would do anything to make sure everyone was happy, and would go out of her way to help anyone even if it was nearly impossible to do.

We were all still sitting on the couch talking when Allison came home from running some errands. After she finished putting things away, I asked her if she could please make homemade bruschetta as an appetizer for everyone. I could tell that my request was putting some pressure on her. When she was preparing it, she made a lot of noise letting me know she wasn't happy. She was almost finished when she had to let her frustration be known. She took us all by surprise when she yelled: "I am doing everything while you just sit there. That is all you do!"

I felt horrible, like she was attacking me for being sick. If she only really knew what I was going through. I tried to share as much as I could with her, but I also didn't want it to be about me in every conversation; therefore, I tried to act as normal as I could. I think once I shared with her that the doctors said this was curable cancer, all her worries went away. She knew that I was going to be fine, and probably expected me to feel at least fine enough to help her in the kitchen.

Within a few minutes, Allison was apologizing to me and telling Steven that the words were really directed toward him. She wanted him to get up from the couch and help make the appetizer, as he was the one resting all morning while she was out grocery shopping. I could tell she really wished Steven had gone with her to help her, and in his defense, he probably would have if she would have asked.

I was glad she voiced this frustration. I could tell it wasn't just frustration from that day, but that it had been building up for days and maybe even weeks. That behavior was so out of character for her. She was always the happy-go-lucky girl. With this coming out so harshly and out of nowhere, it was only a matter of time that it was going to happen.

After Allison apologized, we all enjoyed the yummy bruschetta that she prepared. I could see she was still annoyed with Steven, and that didn't bother him one bit. He actually smiled when she got angry.

"She's a typical teenager, complaining," he whispered to me. "She has an easy and good life. She hasn't done that much, Mom. Most of the errands she did were for herself."

What Steven didn't understand was that this typical teenager was worried about her mom and needed to have some normalcy back in her home. Allison was wishing that with family here, she could have these things. Hopefully with her Aunt Cindy visiting, who was also a mom, things would become easier on Allison.

We all had a lovely remainder of the day reminiscing and hanging out. That evening, Steven and Aunt Cindy cooked dinner together for us all. Unfortunately, dinner didn't stay in me. I was sitting on the couch for only about ten minutes after dinner when it just came out of me without any warning. I was embarrassed and humiliated that this happened in front of family.

I picked myself slowly up off of the couch, hoping it would all stay in my underwear and not come out of my pants. I began to cry. Cindy said, "it's okay, Deb." I could tell by the tone of her voice she felt bad for me. I made it to the bathroom and had to clean this awful and disgusting mess. Once my clothes were off, I had to rinse them off in my toilet and then myself off in the shower. Anything that was salvageable I placed in the laundry.

Not only had this taken everything out of me, leaving me weak and exhausted, it emotionally depressed me. This event was so demoralizing that it made me lose my dignity. How could I leave the house when I had no warning this was going to come out? How can I have anyone come over to visit me? I couldn't imagine this happening in front of my friends. Even though I knew they might want to come and support me, I had to say no. I was in survival mode now. There was no way I would take a chance of this happening around anyone else. It was bad enough in front of family.

As I was taking care of myself, Cindy and Steven made a plan that they would go to the grocery store tomorrow after my treatments and pick up food for the week. Cindy made meal plans and thought of other foods that I could eat that would help with my severe diarrhea. She asked me if I would feel more comfortable wearing depends when we had to leave the house, and she would be happy to pick some up for me. *Oh my goodness!* I thought. *Is this really happening to me?* I wasn't ready to go there, so I told her no, but I thanked her for thinking of the option for me.

Everyone went to bed early that night, because my episode had changed the mood in the room. Everyone felt bad, and none of us had much to say, and it was too late for us to start a movie. Allison gave Steven a big hug goodbye; she would not see him tomorrow because after school she was going to her dads for a couple of days.

Cindy would sleep with me in my California king bed. I didn't want to have Allison give up her room when she had to get up at 5:30 a.m. for school, and the other room was already occupied by my son. He had all his things arranged around the room. This was our arrangement for two days, and after Steven left Cindy could take his room. Besides, I enjoyed having her in the room with me. We would have some alone time to talk, which we did until our eyes couldn't stay open any longer.

13

EXHAUSTED, HUMILIATED. . .
BUT POSITIVE

I didn't eat anything and only drank water the next morning. I decided to limit myself to water only, and not drink any more tea since tea was a diuretic. Knowing that I didn't have control over my bowels, I didn't want to eat anything before we left for my treatments, especially after what had happened last night. I had so much fear that I could have an accident in the car or even walking into the center where others would witness such a tragedy.

Steven drove, showing Cindy the way to both treatment centers. We explained to her that today I would get my labs done at one center, see Dr. Stephanie, then drive to the next center for my radiation. I was glad that this was our schedule so Cindy could have the comfort of sitting with Steven as I had these things done and they could have some time alone.

Steven pulled up to the cancer center and dropped Cindy and I off. He decided to run a quick errand and said to text him when I was done. First we signed in, then walked a few steps to the lab center. Cindy sat in the waiting room as they drew my blood out of my port. Then we headed to the elevator to the second floor to meet with Dr. Stephanie.

It was nice that Cindy was able to meet my doctor. I wanted her to see how nice and compassionate Dr. Stephanie was. I was proud of how she worked with me, observing so closely on how I was feeling and watching my platelets weekly and making the call for my upcoming treatments.

She asked how I was doing with my diarrhea, and I told her that I felt that it was continually getting worse. I mentioned how I lost total control of my bowels last night. Dr. Stephanie shared that she already received my lab results from the blood that I gave downstairs, and that my platelets had jumped up to 123.

Oh no, I thought. *This means I will need to start my chemo pills again, which will add more stomach cramping and diarrhea.*

Dr. Stephanie either read my mind or I must have had a panicked look on my face because she immediately said, "Debra, we will not be doing anymore chemo treatments. Your body can't handle it with the severe diarrhea you're having. We want to try to lessen this so that your body can retain any nutrition that you're eating."

Her words gave me hope that my diarrhea would lessen.

"You will continue with receiving the radiation treatments only," Dr. Stephanie added, and I immediately felt a sense of relief go through me.

"Can we schedule my port removal now, since I will no longer have any chemo?" I asked.

Dr. Stephanie shook her head and said no.

I believe in the power of the mind," I replied, "And by taking out this port, it tells my mind, soul, and body that I no longer need this. My treatments are over and complete."

My doctor looked at me for a moment, then she said, "I don't see why it is necessary to keep it in. I will put the order in for you to have this done. You will receive a call to schedule it."

I was elated by her response.

She continued by asking for me to please stay in touch with her so she could know how I was doing, and if I had any questions I could email her on the patient portal. I had emailed her several other times with issues like fever, what food to eat, and bowel issues, so I knew that she would be respond to me right away if I needed anything like she had in the past. She also said she wanted to see me back in four weeks to take more labs and to see how I was doing a few weeks after all my treatments were completed.

Before we left, I thanked Dr. Stephanie for her guidance and for holding my hand each step of the way. I appreciated how compassionate she was with me through this scary, painful, and horrific experience of all the unknowns. I had tears as I was saying these words. She reached over and handed me some tissue, then smiled and gave me a big hug.

"Debra, you're welcome. You handled this all so gracefully."

As I was walking out of the room, I thought to myself, *Wow! My platelets had jumped up to 123*. It was only four days ago when they were at seventy-six. I was surprised that they went up this high so quickly. I was also so grateful that they went up after the push day and not before. Thank you, God!

Once again, I was seeing how He was working behind the scenes. He knew what was best for me, keeping my platelets low so that I didn't receive my last infusion. Seeing the timing of this and that they jumped up forty-seven points in just four days validated to me that this was all part of His plan.

I saw Steven parked in the nearby parking lot. It only took a few minutes after I texted him for him to pull up to the curb to take us to the next center for my radiation treatment.

The nurses at the radiation center let Steven and Cindy walk back into the room where I received my radiation. They showed them the machine, described how it worked, and how I laid on the table. It was very kind of them to do this for them, as they had already done this for Brad. I could tell by my sister's reaction that she felt the same way that I did the first time I saw the huge machine. It was very intimidating.

When we were finished, Steven asked if it was okay if he stopped at the comic store to purchase a few more books for him and his daughter on the way home. Both Cindy and I said sure. I figured since I had not eaten anything, I would be fine.

The comic store was about ten minutes away, and Cindy waited with me in the car. After fifteen minutes, my stomach began to start cramping.

"Oh no!" I groaned. "Do you see a place that I could run in to use the restroom?"

We glanced around but didn't see anything that was walkable. I texted Steven, but he wasn't responding. Cindy decided to run in and tell him that we needed to go. When she came back in the car, and said he would hopefully be out soon. That "soon" seemed forever when I was in panic mode and felt that I needed to use a restroom soon.

We noticed a bagel store across the street. We had wanted to stop at one on the way home to pick up bagels for everyone for the morning, so this was perfect. I quickly ordered some bagels and left them at the counter to order more as I ran to the restroom. Whew. . .it was a good call, and just in time.

Steven and Cindy were patiently waiting for me, and knew as soon as they saw me, they knew to get up from their seats and move quickly to the car. All I wanted to do was to lie down and curl up in a fetal position. I was feeling humiliated, but was also grateful that we were the only ones in the restaurant.

The radiation treatments were really taking a toll on my body. I understood now how the doctors felt it wasn't good for my body to introduce the chemo pills back into my regiment. I knew from now on after radiation that I would need to go directly home. I didn't want to take any chances not making it home.

It was Steven's last night in town. He had an early flight out the next morning. The three of us decided to grill some portabello stuffed mushrooms, zucchini, and onions, and serve them with French bread. Grilling stuffed portobello mushrooms was a first for them both.

Cindy prepared all the food, Steven did the grilling, and I sat on the couch. Dinner tasted delicious, but I only ate a few bites of everything because I didn't want to overexert my stomach, which seemed to work as I had no issues. I wasn't surprised, as I can't imagine I had much left in me from everything that exploded out of me that afternoon.

We sat at the table talking, with Cindy and Steven sharing a bottle of cabernet. All of us laughed for over an hour, and I knew then that I'd never forget that night.

We discussed how it would be fun to have a family gathering once my treatments were finished, and we aimed for July if the doctors still felt that I would be fine around kids. Steven spoke to his wife, and they offered to throw a celebration for me "kicking cancer's butt" at their home. Their home was large enough to host our entire family, plus my sister and her husband. This was a big commitment, not only for Steven and his family, but for the rest of us as we each would have the expense of flying to get to his home. This was also something for me to look forward to. Another goal for me: to make it through the finish line cancer free.

I was keeping positive. My cancer would be cured, but there were times when my humanness would get the best of me. That usually happened right after I got sick.

I slept well, and morning came quickly. While everyone was busy doing their own thing, I decided I needed to pray. Today I wanted to say goodbye to my cancer pills.

I carried all of my cancer pill bottles that were in one big box into my room where I said my prayers. Each bottle held sixty pills, and I had a total of 540 pills, minus the ones I had already taken. I placed them down on the table next to the picture of Jesus that was hung on my wall where I liked to stand to pray. When looked at this picture, I felt God through Jesus' eyes.

When I prayed, I felt a direct connection. I felt emotions, and the face would change forms: serious, smiling, contentment, pride, and a feeling of love would go through my body each time. This love was a chill that started from the top of my shoulders and traveled down my back all the way down to my toes. It was God's way of telling me He was with me. He heard me, and I was never alone.

I started by holding one pill bottle and ended by holding the entire box of pills with two hands, reaching up in front of my picture. This represented that I was giving these pills to God. They were no longer a part of my life. I was saying goodbye to them.

My Goodbye Prayer to my Chemo Pills

As I held the bottles of chemo pills in my hands, I raised them up and said:

"Thank you, chemo pills, for the work you have done in destroying the cancer that is within my body. God, I am forever grateful for these pills, as this was part of what my body needed to heal. God, you have shown me that my body has had enough of these chemo pills, as my body can no longer handle taking them. God, please help my body get rid of the toxins from these pills., Help my body rebalance and renew my brain from all the side effects.

"Thank you for your guidance and awareness. Even though I am not finishing the remainder of these pills, I trust that I had the exact amount needed and that I need no more to become healthy, whole, and cancer free."

I placed the bottle back into the box with the others. Then I took the entire box and held it in front of God, saying:

"Chemo pills, I am saying goodbye, as I no longer need you. You have done your job. I am placing you in front of God, releasing and surrendering that you are no longer a part of my life and never will be again."

After this prayer, I felt really good. I had a knowingness inside that all was well, all would be well, and so it is.

When I walked into the kitchen, Cindy had just finished getting ready for the day and Steven was finishing some work on his computer before it was time for him to leave. They had both had their bagel for breakfast. Steven's phone beeped with a text from JT that he was sitting outside, ready to take him to the airport. Steven quickly put away his computer, placed his phone in his pocket, and told us he had to go.

I went up to my son and gave him a hug. "I'm so grateful for all of your help. Thank you for leaving your work and family to take care of me. I'm glad we got to share some time together. I'll see you soon." I kissed him on the cheek.

"Mom, I love you," Steven replied, then he gave his Aunt Cindy a hug and said, "If you need anything, let us know. Keep in contact with me on how she is doing. Thank you for being here with her. It makes it easier for me to leave knowing she has you here."

As Steven walked out the door, I couldn't hold back my emotions. This was another part of my healing and dealing with cancer that had come to an end. I felt that what we shared will never be lost, and was something we would always remember; the good and the bad. It was a chapter in our lives that I wished we didn't have to experience, but at the same time it gave us a gift of time with one another that I would always cherish.

My sister and I had the remainder of the morning to hang out and relax. My radiation treatment was not until 2:30. We headed outside to enjoy some sunshine. I grabbed my water and she grabbed her coffee. The warm sun and light conversation felt good. It was just what I needed.

That afternoon was Cindy's first time driving me for treatment. She seemed very relaxed, and we enjoyed our time together even if it was in the car. We always valued our time together, no matter what we were doing, as we didn't get to see each other very often.

When we arrived, I saw that the nurses were worried about how I was feeling. I was walking very slowly, as it was taking so much of my energy to make it to the radiation room. When I was finished, they each told me to go home and rest for the remainder of the day, which I did.

The following day, I looked at my calendar and beamed with excitement. "Cindy," I began happily, "I have exactly one week left! Five more treatments after today until my completion day!"

It seemed like it took forever to get to that week. Time was going so slow. My life had come to a stop, and I was surviving just to make it through each day.

My calendar was helping me get through each day by counting down the days. I was seeing an end to these brutal treatments. Cindy was happy, too. "Deb," she said, "you're almost there. You can do it!"

Thank God I had her around. She was going to hold my hand these next few days, walking through the finish line with me. I would need her to lean on.

As I waited in the waiting room with Cindy to be called in for my radiation treatment, all I could think was, *please, let's get this done with so I can go home and sleep.* The nurse took one look at me and walked over to assist me. She let me lean against her as she walked back to the room. My body was weak and it took so much energy to talk. I was getting undressed and slowly getting myself onto the the radiation table. For the first time, the nurses had to help me.

As they were positioning my body, they said with a sadness in their eyes that they were so sorry for the way I was feeling. I couldn't help but cry. "I'm so sorry," I said through my tears. "I want to be stronger, but can't help it. This is taking everything I have out of me." I cleared my throat, determined to stay positive. "Girls," I added, "I only have five more treatments. I am almost done."

The same nurse assisted me in walking back to Cindy in the waiting room. Cindy had a worried look on her face. I shared with her how kind and compassionate the three nurses were. You could tell they loved their job and gave each of their patients the love that they needed. I sure felt loved by them and I hoped they felt the love I had for each of them, too.

The remainder of the day I rested on the couch. Cindy prepared dinner for her and Allison. All I wanted was water. I felt bad that I was not able to help in the kitchen with the cooking or cleaning up. It was something that I had to let go. If I tried to assist, I would use the energy that I needed for simple tasks like walking to the bathroom, sitting up, and talking.

Illness was consuming my body, and its discomfort was taking over, so all I could do was tend to my broken body. Where was my soul during this time? I discovered my soul had not abandoned me: it was allowing the illness to transform me from the outside in.

Cindy had washed the sheets from the spare room and moved all of her things over. As much as I was sad that she wasn't going to be in my bed with me, I was glad that she was going to have her own space. Now she could relax and do whatever she wanted to do without Allison and I being around her the entire time. Once she finished getting settled in, we all sat on the couch, watching HGTV before going to bed early.

14

UNEXPECTED NEWS: TRUSTING MY DOCTOR

Cindy and I decided that we should play Yahtzee and backgammon. These were two games we played a lot together throughout the years. We were very competitive, and she always said that I was the lucky one and won all the time, which wasn't true.

That comment made us put our game faces on. There was no fooling around. We played backgammon on the back patio in the gorgeous morning weather. The birds were chirping loudly, and Cindy was glad to be here as the weather was much warmer than back in our hometown in Wisconsin.

We always played the best out of three games, and she beat me two out of three. At the end of playing these games, I needed to go back inside and rest on the couch. I couldn't believe this simple, fun task took all my energy. I needed to gain more back to make it to my radiation treatment.

As we walked in the doors of the treatment center, a nurse was waiting there to greet us. She told us that Dr. Steven wanted to see me before treatment today. I thought to myself, *that's odd. He always saw*

me after my treatments. All I could think was that he had a full schedule and was trying to fit all of his work in. She took us immediately
back to a room where we waited for the doctor.

When Dr. Steven greeted Cindy and I, his face was very serious.
I felt nervous, because this wasn't the norm; he usually had a smile
and skip in his step when he entered the room. If I felt bad, he always
changed my attitude around in knowing I was doing well. He had a
way of making me feel better, and I believed in him. I had gained a
huge respect and trust in this doctor.

"This is my sister, Cindy," I began, making the introduction.

Dr. Steven finally smiled. "Have I met your entire family?" he said
in a joking voice, "or is there more that I will get the privilege to meet?"

As he sat in the stool facing my chair, he said, "How are you feeling, Debra?"

"Not very well," I replied honestly. "I could be better."

Dr. Steven nodded. "Debra," he began seriously, "how would you
feel if you didn't have a treatment tomorrow?"

I stumbled answering, as I was confused. Why would we skip a
treatment? Would this mean I would only have four more days left
still having my completion day on April 10th?

After asking him these questions, he replied, "No, Debra. This
would mean we would add this day to next week and have your completion day on April 11th.

"Well, the 10th is the day I have been counting down to," I shared
with him. "It would be hard to add another day to my calendar.
I would rather do the treatment tomorrow and finish this week."

I think he had hoped that I would have taken him up on his sug-
gestion. "The reason I'm saying this is your body has gone through a
lot and is very weak. I do not want you to have treatment tomorrow.
I feel it is best that you take tomorrow off and rest through the weekend. You will be able to handle treatment next week better if you do."

As I looked at Dr. Steven, I knew that he was saying this because he knew what was best for me, so I took his advice. I really didn't think I had the choice; he was telling me in a nice way that this was the way it was going to be.

"I asked Dr. Stephanie if I could schedule my port to be taken out," I said, "and she said yes, but that I want to confirm this with you that is okay."

"No, Debra. I would rather you wait to have this removed after I see you on your next visit on May 10th."

I didn't understand his reasoning, but I trusted him. I figured it was only a month away. I could wait until after the 10th to have it removed.

I had one more question before we left: "Dr. Steven, how do you feel about me traveling to see my children and grandkids in July? How long would you recommend me going for?"

"You should feel fine to travel by mid July," he replied. "It will be nice for you to be around all of your family. I would limit your travel to no more than five days. The plane travel alone is going to wear you out, plus your not used to being around all of your family and grandkids. You are not going to get the same rest as you do when your at home."

I nodded, letting him know that I understood.

He told Cindy it was nice meeting her and thanked her for taking such good care of me. I thought this was very kind of him to say. The nurse came to take me back for treatment.

They were also concerned, and told me I had to slow down. Now I was looking as bad on the outside as I was feeling on the inside. They noticed my worn out, pale, and drawn body. My body temperature was low and my bones hurt.

The nurses knew the adjustment Dr. Steven had made, and they expressed how this was going to be better for me. They reasoned that it really wasn't one more day, it was just moving the completion day by one day. The amount of treatments would be the same.

I was saddened by this news, but I had to accept it and move forward. Looking at my calendar when I got home made me even more sad. If I had completed this full week of treatments, it would leave me only three days left next week. Three days seemed so much easier than four. Looking at four made it seem like there was another full week that I had to complete. Depression set in, and I was frustrated with my body.

Over the weekend, we played many games of Yahtzee and back-gammon. There was no one that I liked to play these two games with more than my sister. We share so many laughs in each game that was played. Over that visit she was the champion of all champions in both Yahtzee and backgammon. I let her be the winner by saying she had an advantage over me. I used the excuse that I was struggling with chemo brain. We both laughed. I was seeing that my chemo brain fog was getting better since I stopped chemo treatment. I found that the days that I pushed myself more were the days that I struggled the most.

I was witnessing that Dr. Steven was right; I needed these days to rest. I was feeling stronger after each day of full rest. I also believed that the laughter that I shared over the weekend with Cindy was also a good part of my healing process. We spent Friday and Saturday evenings searching for movies and watching some of the dumbest and most boring of them together. We always held out, watching each to the end hoping the movie would get better. Each time we started a new one, we laughed and said it had to be better than the last one. We didn't have much success in the movie we chose.

Sunday I decided I wanted to try and get out of the house. We needed a few items at the grocery store, and I felt this would be a quick turn around. It wouldn't be too hard or too long of a time away from the house. My food had been digesting well. The extra carbs that I was adding to my diet, along with having a break from radiation, was helping me not only gain some energy back, but it was also helping me get some nutrition in my body.

Getting in and out of the car was more work than I had expected. My body wasn't used to much exercise. I had been laying down all week-end and resting, following my doctor's orders. Walking into the grocery store, I had to grab onto a cart. I was out of breath And held back my tears. I could not believe this was so hard. I felt like a weak ninety-nine year old woman. I felt like I was dizzy and was going to faint. I knew that this dizziness was a sign that I wasn't drinking enough water.

Cindy raced around the store, grabbing all the items we needed to make our trip go as quickly as possible. She was so kind and caring. I know she was as shocked as I was with how bad I was doing in the store.

On our way back home, she expressed that from now on she was fine with going to the store without me. I also mentioned that we could send Allison if we needed something. This was an eye-awakening experience. I realized how bad I truly was, and how much my body was enduring.

It made me grateful for the little things that I could still do. I was finding myself feeling joy in folding the blanket on the couch, throwing a load of laundry in, or even being able to take a shower, as at times these tasks were almost impossible to do.

This lesson taught me that no matter how difficult a day was or whatever I was going through to find one piece of joy in that day. That lesson was something that I continued to use daily.

On Monday, we didn't need to get my labs drawn like we usually did. It was going to be an easy week because we only had to drive to one treatment center. The rest I received over the weekend helped my bowels get back on track. I was feeling positive that I could make it through my last four treatments without going backward. Time would tell, as the radiation always seem to have its own agenda.

The nurses were so pleased to see how well I was doing since last Thursday. I was back to having some color in my face, walking on my own and I was joyful. Treatment went by fast, and before long we were back on the road heading home. I was enjoying all of the smells from the restaurant that we drove by. I even said to Cindy that if I felt this good on Completion Day, we should go out to an early happy hour. This was a complete turn around. I was feeling safe enough with my bowels to go out and eat at a restaurant. I knew that I wouldn't be able to stay out long, but it felt good to feel somewhat normal.

We were in downtown Scottsdale, in the center of all the restaurants. It was baseball season, so there were a lot of vacationers in town. The streets were crowded and the patios were full of groups of people all happy and celebrating. Driving by this scene many times, I would say, "I wish I could go back to the days when I didn't have a care in the world. These people don't know how lucky they have it. They are walking around exploring, laughing, and hanging out." That was the life! I couldn't wait to do this again. Now, I saw life through a different lense. I looked forward to the day that I would feel normal again and could spend an entire day out. I would be so grateful and blessed to do these simple acts of joy.

My countdown had begun! I only had two more days left before Completion Day. I never thought this day would come. Over the last two and a half months, I felt like I had lost a part of my life. When I looked back, it felt like those days didn't exist. It was hard for me to even believe that it was already April. At the same time, it also felt that each day was going by so slowly. I had looked forward to my final week, and now it was here. Crazy as both scenarios sounded, that was exactly how I felt.

During the last week, I saw how the laughter that I was sharing with Cindy and Allison was a key part of my healing process. It took the heaviness of each hardship that I went through and made it lighter. With every chance I had, I chose to not let myself stay in depression and moved forward from it more easily. I looked forward to whatever we were going to do, whether it was our time spent outside relaxing, making dinner, playing games, watching movies, or just hanging out. I was replacing the worry, stress, and pain with joy and being present in that joy that my family was surrounding me with.

On our way home on Wednesday from radiation, I asked Cindy if she could stop by Trader Joes. I wanted to pick up a few food items and plants to give to the nurses on my last day. There were many plants to choose from. I decided to purchase individual rose plants for each of the girls instead of one set of roses. That way, they could each take a rose plant home.

I wanted this to be a reminder of the impact they made on my life. I chose one yellow, one pink, and one peach set of mini rose bushes that were each planted in beautiful pots. I had an idea of which color I would give to which nurse, thinking which one they would like the best. We would see if I was right on Thursday.

It was getting hard to watch my sister always preparing and making our dinners. I wanted to help, but I also didn't want to use my energy. I needed to conserve it to help my body heal. Cindy understood and never made me feel like I was taking advantage of her. I made sure she always had a glass of wine as she was preparing food or while we ate dinner. This made me feel better, knowing she was able to enjoy something while she was working.

The night before April 11th, I went to bed with a happy spirit. I was excited that tomorrow was Completion Day. We were going to celebrate the entire day! I could hardly wait. The next morning, I was very overwhelmed. This was such a powerful day. I did it! I made it through my treatments! I was so proud of myself and thankful for everyone that helped me reach that day. I was going to place the last star on my calendar.

Amy called to congratulate me, and she wanted to stop before we left for my final radiation treatment. I was receiving many phone calls and my door bell was ringing with all the gifts that were being sent. I was touched from the abundance of love I was shown. I knew everyone was celebrating me, but they were also celebrating the day where they would no longer have to see me go through so much pain. This was also a day they were all looking forward to as well.

I was so proud of this accomplishment that I wanted to make sure I took pictures with the beautiful calendar that Erin had made for me, because it had helped me in so many ways.

Me standing next to my calendar with the many gifts I received.

Amy and I

Patty and I

My sister Cindy and I

This beautiful flower arrangement was sent from Cindy's husband, Jim. The flowers were purple and white. He chose the purple ones to remind me of my mother in Heaven. The words he wrote on the card put Cindy and I into tears. We both felt the love and compassion he was sending me.

My morning was filled with so many joyful moments. I was grateful to everyone who made this day special and unforgettable.

15

April 11, 2019

Cindy and I placed the three roses from Trader Joe's into the car and headed to the radiation center. I felt a bit anxious and liberated knowing this was my final radiation treatment. It had been a long six weeks of making these trips to these doctor appointments every day. I was looking forward to having my days back.

In the past, I hated giving up a day to go to any kind of health appointment. Now, I would be grateful for going to these appointments, knowing they were only taking up a portion of one day and not an entire day or month. This had changed my entire way of thinking about doctor appointments.

I would not see Dr. Steven that day like I usually do on every Thursday. He told me in my last appointment he was going to miss Completion Day as he would be on vacation in Maui. Wow, that sounded so lovely and peaceful, I decided to make it a goal of mine: I would go to Maui soon. The next time I would see him would be May 10th.

During that visit, I had asked Dr. Steven what I should expect on the upcoming weeks. What would my healing be like? Would my symptoms continue to get worse? When should my healing begin where I would start to feel better?

His reply was, "Every person is different; some can handle this pain where others will feel this is extreme pain. Early side effects occur immediately after treatments, but they're typically gone within one to two weeks after treatment ends. You may feel some fatigue, diarrhea, weakness, discomfort during bowel movements, and anal irritation."

He let me know that radiation would continue working after my last treatment and I may experience these issues for a two to three weeks, or even months after. I needed to be aware of lower energy levels, inflammation in the anus, which may cause bleeding and pain, blisstering on the outer anal wall, mucus or blood in your stool, vaginal dryness, and abnormal swelling in the legs, called lymphedema. He also mentioned skin changes, like dryness, itching, and peeling.

Dr. Steven shared that my energy would increase over time, and my body would not be back to its normal self till about from one year from the date I started radiation, which was on March 28, 2019. He reminded me to not be hard on myself, and to see my rectal doctor to determine a follow up care plan of rectal exams so that she can monitor the inside walls of my rectum and anal canal. She would watch for any abnormal changes, and Dr. Steven would follow up with her. I could return to work as soon as I felt up to it.

He put in an order for me to have a PetScan on July 8th, saying he liked to wait several months after treatment ended to allow the radiation to continue to kill the cancer cells. When I saw him in a month, I would set up a time to have my port removed.

I made a mental log of all of these symptoms Dr. Stevens mentioned that may or may not occur. This gave me the awareness of what to watch out for, and that if anything occurred, it was normal. I would have to see what each day would bring, and take it day by day.

In the meantime, I prayed daily, asking God to help heal these symptoms. I asked that they wouldn't occur, but if they did that they would be lessened. If any should arise that were extremely difficult, I would let go and let God take over. I trusted that my healing was in His hands.

MY DAILY PRAYER

"I place this pain and worry in your hands. Please, God, heal this now, as I no longer want to feel this or need it. Take it away and allow me to be healthy and whole now. Please comfort me during these painful times. Thank you, God."

I was excited to see my three nurses and give them their roses. I wanted them to know how much I appreciated all that they had done for me. We walked back to the radiation room, and I placed all three of the rose pots on the check-in counter. The nurses were so happy. They each greeted me with a hug.

I decided that rather than give out the roses to each nurse, I would let them pick the color (pink, yellow, or peach) that they wanted. It was fun to watch as they conversed which ones they thought they liked best. Each nurse picked the same color flowers that I originally was going to give them. Spirit was guiding me and had guided them.

I shared with them that these roses could be planted in the ground, so each year when they bloomed they could remember me and the gratitude I had for all the love I felt from them.

As I laid on the radiation table for the last time, I felt empowered. I did it!

The nurse that always placed the warm, white blanket on me said, "This is bittersweet, Debra. I am happy for you that this is your last day, but I am going to miss placing this white blanket on you every-day. I am going to miss you."

My radiation nurses and me on Completion Day.

Her comment was so sweet. I would never forget the compassion that these ladies gave to me each and every day. They became part of my Army. Their positive attitude, love, and compassion helped give me the strength I needed to go through my daily radiation treatments, especially toward the end when it was getting tough. They were my cheerleaders each week, saying, "how was your weekend? How are you feeling? You are one day closer, Debra."

It felt good leaving. I told Spirit and God thank you for these treatments, but for the rest of my life I never wanted to have radiation again.

Cindy and I were ready to find a place close for lunch. We drove around the corner and found a place to park the car. We walked a few blocks, deciding which restaurant we wanted to eat at. I was getting sore from walking, and we had to make a decision quickly or I may have had to go back to the car. We chose the "Herb Box", as it had a lovely patio and there were fewer people there than at other restaurants. This was most likely because we were eating such a late lunch and also because it was just the beginning of Happy Hour at 3:00 p.m.

We chose our table on the patio and changed our minds two times until we found the perfect seats where we would be out of the sun. We had the patio to ourselves most of the time that we were there. There were only two other tables occupied by the time we left. It was hard to believe that I felt good enough to go out to eat.

I was careful with what I ordered in the hopes that it would not bother my stomach. Cindy and I shared a few items off of the Happy Hour menu; a beet salad and ribs, which Cindy had all to herself as the only meat I ate was chicken. We also shared their gluten free butternut squash and corn enchiladas. It was the perfect amount as we each had one. I had eaten there before and this was my favorite dish. I was so excited for Cindy to try it. She enjoyed it as much as I did.

It was wonderful to be able to do something fun with Cindy. All she had been doing was taking care of me and hanging around the house. I knew this was going to be as good for her as it was for me. Having this luncheon lifted both of our spirits. This was the beginning of me telling cancer that I had enough of it controlling my life. I wanted to go back to my normal life.

Back at home we continued our celebration day enjoying the rest of the beautiful weather by relaxing on the couch in the backyard. I continued to get calls from family congratulating me on my accomplishment. The Facetime calls with my grandkids were the best.

Seeing them always made my days better. They brought laughter and love to me with each call.

Prior to going to bed that night, I sat in prayer giving thanks to God for all that he had done for me.

My Gratitude Prayer

"Thank you, God, for this day and for giving me the strength to make it through these rigorous and painful thirty days. Please continue giving me strength, courage, and healing in the remaining days, weeks, and months of my healing process. I know that you have been healing me each step of the way, as I was told early on that this could have been so much worse. I give gratitude for this and for where I am today. Thank you for your guidance and for always being at my side. Amen. All is well, all will be well, and so it is."

That night I knew I would sleep well. One weight was lifted from me. I no longer had to feel the stress of making it to and from my appointments, and wondering what side effects I would feel from each treatment that I received. That process was done! Allelujah!

Cindy had five more days with me before she went home. That meant we would have five days of no treatments and no commitments! We could enjoy each day with each other, and we did this the best that we could due to my unsettling circumstances.

We played endless games of Yahtzee, Backgammon, and watched movies. This seemed to be our trend of things to do with my limitations. We planned healthy meals along with good wine for her to enjoy with every dinner. Anything from this point on might be difficult, but I had to keep my mind focused that there would be an end in sight.

I was eating more and getting my bowels in check little by little. I wasn't getting the uncontrollable severe diarrhea like I had previously. However, I never knew which foods may or may not cause me to have a flare up. If we had somewhere we needed to go, I limited the amount of food I ate and I took out all fiber and dairy from my diet.

Having radiotherapy to my lower lymph nodes in my groin meant the area between my hips, pelvic area, and/or abdomen could have side effects. I took sitz baths daily to relieve the irritation, inflammation, and pain. Radiation was like having a very bad sunburn, and trust me, that wasn't a spot where anyone wanted to have a sunburn.

It made it very painful to go to the bathroom. Often times I thought, *well, if I don't eat, I won't have to go.* I was feeling the side effects from the radiation more and more each day. Dr. Steven did share with me that I would feel the worst from my radiation for a few weeks after it was completed before it would start to feel better. He also told me that radiation continued to work for months after treatments.

Allison was at her dad's for the weekend and called to say she was going prom dress shopping with her friend. Later that night she called again from the mall, very excited that she found a dress. I told her to ask a person that worked there if they could take my credit card over the phone. Unfortunately, they could not and would not make any exceptions.

I told her to put the dress on hold and go back and pick it up tomorrow with my credit card. She placed the dress on hold, but she told me that there was no way she would be able to pick the dress up tomorrow, as she had to work the entire day and it being Sunday, the mall would be closed when she got off.

Cindy and I decided we would take on the task of picking up Allison's prom dress tomorrow. It was the last one in her size, and they would only hold it for twenty-four hours. We really didn't have any other choice.

We planned on leaving in the afternoon to the mall, as this would give us a lazy morning to enjoy hanging outside, and for Cindy to enjoy this beautiful weather. It was snowing in Wisconsin, so she was soaking as much sun up as she could before she left.

I decided to be the one that drove to the mall. It as about a forty-five minute drive. This was the first time I drove since my treatments started in February. I figured I should drive when I had Cindy in the car with me for the first couple of times. That way, if I felt I was having problems, I could pull over and let her drive. Driving felt good. This now gave me the freedom to come and go when I chose, and not be limited to having others help take me places or pick things up from the grocery store for me.

I hadn't been to that particular mall in years. I wasn't sure where the store was located in the mall and took a guess on where to park. Walking into the mall, Cindy and I found a map to locate where we were and where the store was. It turned out I could not have picked a farther parking garage! We had to walk across the entire mall to get to this store. I laughed and told Cindy this would be a test to see how well I did, and it would be good exercise, too.

We got half way and I had to stop to rest. I was out of breath and my heart rate was elevated. I was surprised and disappointed to see how quickly my body tired out. Before I started chemo and radiation therapy, I worked out every day and I was in good shape. My body wasn't as strong as I thought it was anymore.

By the time we made it to the store, I was exhausted. Once we purchased the dress, I told Cindy I needed to walk slower. I felt like I was going to faint, but I didn't want to make Cindy nervous and I didn't want to pass out in the store. That would be so embarassing. I took a deep breath and I concentrated on each step. As soon as we exited the store, Cindy saw an escalator to the left that would take us down a level where she saw some chairs.

My heart was pounding and beating so fast that it made my body shake. Cindy held my arm to help stabilize me as she guided me to the chairs. "Deb, do you need me to get help?" she asked as she sat next to me.

I shook my head. "I wanted to take my pulse," I told her. "Can you keep time on your watch and let me know when a minute is over?"

Oh my. . .this wasn't good! My heart rate was extremely high at 160 beats per minute. I knew I would be okay once I could get it down. I had this happen to me before, so I knew what to do. I put my head down between my knees and took deep breaths until my heart reset back to a slower rate. When that happened, it made the body feel like it had just run a marathon. It wiped me out.

Walking back to the car seemed to take forever. Walking was becoming painful. I could feel the inflammation of my anal wall. It felt as if my butt cheeks were rubbing together every step I took. The skin between my inner butt cheeks was peeling, dry, red, and sore. This sensation was extremely painful. Another way I could describe it was it felt like I had a dry tampon that was improperly placed, causing friction every time I took a step.

I was taking baby steps and wondering if others could tell that I was walking funny or in pain. I tried my best to walk upright and to talk with Cindy as much as I could, making myself look less obvious. I was walking with gratitude that I was making it and that my heart rate was staying in check.

Cindy was very kind to have carried the long prom dress draped over her arm the entire way to the car. She hung the dress on the hook in the backseat and asked me if I wanted her to drive. I felt confident that once I sat down, my pain would greatly diminish to were I would be fine to drive. It would also take my mind off of my pain.

Allison was very thankful that we did this for her. Explaining what we went through to get the dress didn't have the same impact as it did going through it. Who would have thought that picking up a prom dress would have been that difficult and would have taken so long? This will be one experience Cindy and I would never forget.

Larry invited Cindy and I over for dinner. During Cindy's stay, she had met both Larry and Patty. She was always telling me how lucky I was to have two loving, caring neighbors, and that it made her feel better knowing I had them around.

Larry made one of my favorite meals that we had shared together many times: grilled teriyaki boneless skinless chicken thighs, served it with brown rice and asparagus. I know he did this hoping that since this was something I enjoyed, I would be able to eat more.

Larry was also one who enjoyed good wine and had a showcase wine refrigerator to prove it. That night he opened a special bottle to celebrate my completion. I had every intention of having a glass, but when it came down to having one I felt that it would be best for me to wait until I had healed more.

I ate more than I had in a long time, but it must have not looked like that much to both Larry and Cindy, as they kept asking me if I wanted more. I didn't want to push it and eat more where it could cause my stomach to spasm. I was full, and grateful that I was feeling good. It also felt wonderful to be out of my home and eating at a dear friend's house. This was a huge accomplishment for me.

We stayed for a while after dinner. Larry asked Cindy all about her life, we laughed, and shared stories. Before we left, Cindy asked Larry for his chicken recipe, which I said I had and would share with her. We all hugged and Cindy said, "Thank you for watching over my sister."

As she said this, it made me have tears. I could tell it was going to be hard for her to leave, but on the other hand, I thought she was ready to get back home. She had to return to work and her son was going to propose to his girlfriend that following weekend, where he asked her and her husband to be apart of. She had good things to look forward to.

Walking home, I expressed to Cindy how much I loved her and thanked her for going over to Larry's. It was a lovely evening, and I was so thankful that I was able to share it with them.

16

Holding Onto my Knowingness: All Will be Well

The following day, Cindy mentioned going to the grocery store to make sure my house was stocked with food before she left the next day. I wanted to go along, and to make sure I didn't have the same issues as yesterday, I decided to use some lubricating cream the doctor had prescribed to help with my inflammation.

My skin was itchy, and I was noticing that the skin on my entire body was flaking. I was finding tiny, white flecks on the inside of all my clothing. When I got changed, the flakes fell to the floor. This was so strange; I felt like I was shedding.

Thank God they were so tiny that it wasn't causing any visual changes on my skin. After speaking to my doctors, I learned that this was caused from my chemotherapy. Chemo could cause the skin to become dry, cracked, and then peel. It could also happen from dehydration, which I had from the chemotherapy.

I noticed I was getting some of my energy back, and that if I did little things throughout my day, I was able to complete most of everything that I needed to do. These often consisted of driving, cooking less-intensive simple meals, and on a good day maybe finishing one load of laundry, too. I still did not have the strength to clean my house. I had scheduled house cleaners to come when Brad left, and had scheduled their return the day after Cindy would leave.

This would take a lot of pressure off of me. I liked a clean house and knew that it would drive me crazy if my floors or bathrooms were not clean. I knew if I didn't have the cleaners, I would push myself to do the tasks myself, which wouldn't be good and could set me back in my healing process.

I drove to the grocery store with Cindy and then rested the remaining of the afternoon outside. We played a few board games, knowing it would be our last time in a long time before we could play together again. For the first time, I helped in the kitchen preparing dinner, which felt good as I always felt bad that Cindy was the one making dinners while I rested on the couch. One of the lessons I learned with having cancer was to allow others to help me and not be afraid to ask when I needed help.

Our last evening together we spent on the living room couch. Cindy was asking me if I felt well enough to be alone. It has been weeks since I hadn't had someone to talk with, hang out with, or cry to. She wanted to know that if I needed anything someone was right there in my home that could help me. To be honest, I didn't know how I was going to emotionally feel. I knew physically I would be fine now being alone.

At times when my body took over, it became the boss where I couldn't tap into my inner resources. It literally took me to my knees. I was finally back to where I was stronger than my body. I could tell my body what I wanted to get done, but it did still limit me. It let me know when I couldn't deny it when I had no more energy to do anything. That was when I had to honor my body and rest so that it could continue to heal.

I couldn't have made it through the last eighteen days without my big Sis. She came to my rescue. She took over everything that I couldn't do emotionally and physically. She held me up when I couldn't walk. She was my sounding board, my rock, and gave me hope when I didn't have any. What she did for me was out of unconditional love, but was also irreplaceable. She was willing to go into that ugly space with me. I was beyond grateful for her and the love she gave me.

Cindy flight wasn't until 4:00 p.m the following day, and JT would pick her up around 2:30. This gave her plenty of time to shower and pack her belongings. We were able to enjoy one more beautiful morning outside, with Cindy having her coffee with her favorite hazelnut creamer and me with my room temperature water with no ice. Why did it always seem that time went faster the last day one spent with someone that was leaving? I would have loved to have time go slower today.

It was almost time for Cindy to go. Her suitcase and purse were placed by the door. She said her goodbyes to Layla, telling her to be a good dog, behave, and not give me a hard time. Her phone text dinged; it was JT saying he was outside waiting to take her to the airport. We embraced each other and tears began to roll.

There were no more words that we could say, as we had said them all, but the look that we gave one another was of pure love. The one blessing that we each could take from this visit would be the quantity and quality of time we got to spend with one another.

As Cindy walked out the door, she said, "Deb, take care of yourself. Let me know how you are feeling, and please be honest with me. I am always here for you. I love you."

"I will," I replied. "And I love you, too."

Right after she left, I started second-guessing myself. I was now feeling nervous to be alone. The house was really quiet, and I was already starting to feel lonely. I had to replace my quietness with grati- tude. I had to embrace and live in the now. I decided to cuddle up with a blanket on the couch and enjoy the quietness. I looked at it as a gift. I had to enjoy it while I could, as it may only be this way for awhile. I knew it wouldn't be this way forever.

I was witnessing how God worked behind the scenes, guiding my family in arranging the perfect amount of days that each person was with me, and which weeks to come and which week to end on. My family tried their best to work around what my doctors predicted would be my hardest times. Plans were made, flights were sched- uled, and they each took the amount of time that they could off of work.

This was all arranged early on to get the best prices on airfares. From the exact days that my family arrived to the exact days that they left was when I felt my worst to when I was strong enough to be on my own. I call this Divine Planning. I was grateful to my family and to God for being with me and holding my hand through my weak- est, scariest, darkest, and most painful moments that I endured going through my cancer treatments.

I also trusted God's inner guidance that I felt when planning my work schedule. Changing my first schedule wasn't an easy task for Valerie or me. I was trusting my gut feeling when I gave Valerie the dates that I felt I was going to be strong emotionally, physically, and spiritually for my healing sessions. I really had no idea how I would feel. How would I know, when I have never gone through cancer treatments?

That gut feeling I was having was God speaking to me. It was a strong knowing I had within that all would be well by the second week of April. During my entire thirty day chemo and radiation treat- ments, I only took two weeks off. It was amazing how God worked.

I am in awe with how this plan was done weeks prior and how spot on to the day that I was feeling well, just like God had said I would be. God is good!

Over the next few weeks I grew stronger and healthier, starting on April 17th when I went back to work. My sessions were going well and every day I was able to do a little bit more. Allison came home and my cleaning ladies helped keep everything clean. My appreciation grew for the ordinary things I normally took for granted. I was joyful for being able to do even one load of laundry. I was now driving myself to appointments and even going grocery shopping on my own. This was so liberating.

That Sunday was Easter Sunday. It was also the first day that my rose bushes bloomed! I loved my roses and got so much pleasure in seeing them bloom. What were the odds that of all days they would bloom today? I remembered how it took all of my energy the night prior to my first infusion to cut them all back so that I could enjoy them months later. My work paid off! Thank you, God!

What was even more amazing was that I was not only appreciating the beauty from looking at them, but I was able to smell them, too.

Having my sense of smell back to enjoy the beautiful scent from these roses brought joy into my day.

I picked these roses from my rose bushes on Easter Sunday

A few days later, I met my new rectal doctor for the first time. Amy was coming with me to this appointment. I wanted her opinion on how she felt about this doctor after we met her. It was important for me to have a second opinion. I wanted to make sure I would be making the right choice in finding the right rectal doctor.

When we arrived, we sat in the office waiting room for over an hour. I told Amy from the day I scheduled the appointment that I had second thoughts about this office. I had read the reviews that patients were not happy with the office staff, yet I felt I needed to give this doctor a chance, as she was highly recommended by Dr. Stephanie. I also told Amy I wanted a doctor that would have a good eye so that nothing would get overlooked or missed again. Finally, we were called back into a room. When the doctor entered, I had a good feeling about her.

She sat on a stool right in front of me. She asked me to explain my story; what all happened and how it led me to her. After explaining, I told her that I didn't like to talk poorly about my last rectal doctor, as I knew we were all human and we all made mistakes, but I didn't trust her anymore. I didn't want her to think I was jumping from doctor to doctor.

"Debra," the new doctor replied, "This is your body and you have the right to choose the doctor you want for yourself."

"Do you think that my other doctor was wrong by not taking out my hemorrhoid?" I asked. "When I had a previous hemorrhoid that led me to pre-cancerous cells?" I felt she dropped the ball and didn't read my chart when she took over my case when my first rectal doctor left.

She explained that most doctors didn't like to remove hemorrhoids; they would rather leave them in if they were causing no harm. "However," she added, "you were a high-risk patient, so she should have taken this hemorrhoid out."

In my mind, I couldn't help feeling somewhat angry. Had my previous doctor taken the hemorrhoid out back in November when I first came to her about it, I most likely would not have had to go through the intensive treatments that I had. I had to let this anger go, knowing it would not serve me. There was nothing I could do to change what happened.

The new doctor proceeded, saying that she would like to check me, that she had a good eye, and she would watch closely every three months on my changes. Wow! She said the magic words: "I have a good eye!" I knew at that moment she was the doctor for me.

She also stated that she felt it was very important that I only see one doctor, as too many doctors checking this area would not be good. I gave her my word that she would be my only doctor doing the checkups. She asked to take a quick look today, if I could tolerate it. Amy left the room to wait for me.

The exam was brutally painful. The pain was so extreme that I held on tight to the table, and felt many times like I was going to faint. She asked if I wanted to continue or come back in two weeks. In my mind I told myself, *Debra, you don't want to have to do this again in two weeks. You can do this.*

I gave her permission to continue and took several deep breaths to help me get through the pain. When the exam was finished, she told me I was one tough lady. She said she would like to examine me again in three months. We hugged, I got dressed, and then headed out to greet Amy.

"How did it go?" Amy asked right away. "Are you okay?"

"The doctor said everything looked like it should right now," I explained to her as we walked out to the car. "I had a lot of damage on my walls that would come out in the next few weeks. She said not to worry about this and that it was normal. It wasn't an easy exam. It was painful, but I did it."

Amy's looked terrified and replied, "I don't know how you do it, girl. I can't imagine you being examined after all your treatments and that area being so swollen."

"You do what you have to do," I said. We were both relieved that all looked as well as it could right now.

Amy and I discussed on the way home that we both felt really good with this rectal doctor. We were impressed with how she spent over an hour just listening to my story. She made me feel like I mattered and that I was in good hands. I could now rest at peace, knowing I had another doctor whom I trusted as part of my team.

On the 29th, I went to my follow up appointment with Dr. Stephanie. I went through the regular routine of getting my blood work drawn first, though this time it would not be drawn out of my port; it would be taken from my arm. The doctor had ordered it to be drawn this way, as she wasn't sure if I would have had my port removed by now.

It felt strange not having it drawn out of the port, but it also felt good in knowing I was done with this procedure.

I shared with Dr. Stephanie how I was getting my energy level back and that most of the side effects that I had from the chemo were gone. I would go days and even a week without having diarrhea. She shared with me that my platelet count was up to 143, which meant it still wasn't back to my normal count and that I still had a compromised immune system.

I questioned if she thought if my immune system would be strong enough for me to fly to and visit my children and grandkids, as they wanted to celebrate the completion of my treatments. She felt I was progressing in the right direction, and that I would be fine booking my reservations for seeing my family in mid to end of July. This news gave me hope in knowing that it would be only a few months before I would start to feel back to normal.

I was staying connected daily with my friends, neighbors, and family over the phone, keeping everyone updated with my healing progress. I spent many hours talking with Jan and with Valerie. This gave me much comfort, especially when I was feeling alone.

I took Layla outside for short walks. I would get to the end of the block and then have to turn around because I either had to go to the bathroom or I felt too weak to continue. I felt bad for her, as she was excited to be out on a walk and then I would have to shorten it. I knew that I needed to build up my stamina, but I also had to take it slow in doing so. I would do this walk daily, adding a few more steps every other day until I could get to the mailbox.

Layla was helping me in my healing process. Knowing she wanted to walk farther pushed me to walk more and more each day. Within a few weeks, I had reached the mailbox, which was about a block and a half from my house. This was a huge accomplishment for me. But I also had to walk back.

After this, I pushed myself little by little to increase my duration. I was seeing improvement, and this gave me incentive to do more. Next, I added weights to my work out. I started with only five pound weights. I couldn't believe how heavy they felt. I was going in the right directions and felt proud of myself for the work I was doing to build up my body and strength.

May 9th was my follow up appointment with Dr. Steven. I wished I could say that the time had gone by fast since my last visit, but it hadn't. From Completion Day on April 11th to then, I was tired every day. This was considered my re-building period, until I would get my next PetScan.

I let Dr. Steven know that I had been working one day a week so far, and still got very tired throughout the day. Over the next month, I was planning on going back to my normal schedule. He had placed an order for my follow-up PetScan, but sometimes insurance didn't approve these scans unless a CT was done first. Either way, I would hear from the same place where my first scan was done during the first week of July. Then, both he and Dr. Stephanie would talk about my future care.

"Dr. Steven," I asked, "you mentioned in our first visit that this was curable. Are you concerned that we did not cure this cancer?"

He said, "Debra, you have done extremely well with your treatments. You handled this all with such grace. Now we have to wait and see what the scans show us. We take one step at a time."

I took a deep breath and said, "I am going to believe that all was healed. I have prayed every step of the way."

I told him I had scheduled my port to be taken out on May 14th, which was the following Tuesday. I now understood why he had me wait; if I would have had it taken out earlier, I would not have had the emotional and physical strength that I did now.

One of the radiation nurses came into the room. She bought me in a selection of gifts to choose from to honor me completing my treatments. I chose a white t-shirt, as I was drawn to the heart and logo "No One Fights Alone". Another validation that they were part of my Army.

My completion of treatment t-shirt gift.

I asked Dr. Steven one more question before I left, to see if he was okay with my travel plans for my celebration with my family in July. He let me know I should be good enough to travel by the third week of July, but that I should limit my trip to five days or so, and did not recommend the ten days that they had offered.

Dr. Steven got up from his chair and gave me a hug. He told me he was proud of how I handled going through my treatments. Having a doctor that had compassion made all the difference in the world. I felt like we got to know each other well over those thirty days, and I told him I felt blessed to have him as my doctor and that he had an amazing team of radiation nurses. He thanked me and also said he felt they were wonderful, too.

Afterward, I met with a friend for lunch that I hadn't seen since my infusion in February. My cancer had gotten in the way of us seeing one another. We had a wonderful lunch and even went into the church "Old Adobe Mission" next door after. It felt powerful being in the church together. It was like everything had come to full completion. He lit a candle for his son in spirit, and I said a prayer in my mind of gratitude for this day. He walked me to my car and we both embraced, knowing we would see each other again soon.

When I returned home, I called my family to let them know both of my doctors had approved my travel. Steven and I argued a bit about the time I would spend, and in the end we agreed that we would plan for the third week of July and see who could make it then. I would plan around how long they could stay. I went to bed that night telling God how grateful I was for that day and for giving me the strength to make it through my treatments that led up to it. My heart was content and I felt my future looked bright. I was ready to live a healthy, happy, joyful life again.

17

—◆—

VICTORY

On the 14th of May, I had my port removed as planned. Later that day, I received an email from "My Chart", which was an account each patient had to view messages from their doctors, check appointments, and more. When I logged in, the message showed me that my results from my labs that were taken prior to my procedure. My platelet count was at 157. I was back to my normal healthy range! I realized right then that this was another reason my radiation doctor wanted me to wait. Had my platelets been too low, they would not have done the surgery.

Everything happened in perfect order. It may not have been the timing I had wanted in the beginning, but I trusted Dr. Steven even though Dr. Stephanie said I could have my port removed right away. I had a strong gut feeling that I should wait, and now I knew why. I was grateful that I trusted my gut, which I called my intuition. Those feelings I got were nudges from Spirit and/or God. I had to listen and trust, and not second-guess myself. When I have listened and trusted, they have never guided me wrong.

I was feeling and witnessing my limitations, which weren't easy to accept. It was hard not to get depressed, but I recognized this was all part of my healing process; I needed to listen to my body and trust what I was feeling, then honor myself to take the time to heal and rest. I had to do my part, just like my doctors and my treatments did theirs. All of this went hand in hand. I witnessed during my healing sessions how God used my chemo-radiated body as a vessel to heal others. My soul took me beyond my physical illness to heal.

Plans were made and I decided to fly out on Saturday the 20th of July, so I could celebrate my granddaughter's fourth birthday and stay for nine days. My energy level was not that high, but Steven reassured me that I would feel the love from everyone and that I would rest at his house. I agreed. I knew I would enjoy being around my grandkids. and it would be better than resting at home alone. I would be surrounded by love, and love heals.

One month before my PetScan, I realized there were days when my humanness would start to take over and I became fearful. My mind would mess with me. *How can I really know if this cancer is still in me or if it has been healed?* I often questioned. *What would I do if my cancer is not healed and gone? What would be my next plan of attack? What would the doctors next plan be for me? Would I even consider doing more radiation and chemo, and would I even be allowed to do more with all the treatments I have had already?*

I knew I needed to turn my fear into faith. I needed to trust God had a plan for me, just like He had a plan for everyone. I decided that whenever I would have these fearful thoughts, I would repeat these words in my mind: *I am healthy, I am whole, God healed me.* When this wasn't enough, I would pray.

TURNING FEAR INTO FAITH PRAYER

"Dear God, I am having fearful thoughts. I place all of my fearful thoughts into your hands. I release this worry, my stress, all of the unknowns, and fear to you, God. I allow you to take full control. This will free me from all of this."

One evening, I heard these words in response to my prayer: "Debra, if a young child would come to you and say 'I am afraid', you would embrace them and tell them it's okay. They would trust you, and in that moment they would feel that everything was okay. I am embracing you, Debra. You are my child." At that moment, I felt a calmness and peace come through me.

I then prayed, asking God to surround my body and the area the cancer was in with His light and love. I prayed that no cancer would show in the PetScan. If it did, it would be localized in an area that could be treated, and it would not have spread. *Let the PetScan reveal that this has been healed through you and the doctors. Thank you, God. Amen.*

As time went by and I continued to heal, I started to appreciate my abilities to do little things that had not brought me joy in the past, like laundry, dusting, and vacuuming. Friends came by to visit, and I slowly learned how to embrace the challenges of my healing process. Before I knew it, my PetScan was the next day, and I said a prayer of gratitude before going to bed, knowing that all would work out as God planned.

I woke up feeling lighter. I didn't feel overwhelmed or stressed. I was trusting the process. God had my back. He would be with me every step of the way today. I was grateful that I remembered not to wear any clothes with zippers or metal on them. This would save me from having to wear those uncomfortable, oversized one size fits all gowns. Today Patty was driving me. I didn't know how I would feel after the scan and felt that I should play it safe and have someone drive me. We left at 7:30 a.m.

After getting into Patty's car, I turned to look at my good friend as we pulled out of my driveway. "You know," I began, "this will take a few hours. You can leave after dropping me off, if you want to."

Patty glanced at me and gave me her angelic smile. "Deb, I'm not leaving you. I'll go grab a coffee across the street, but I'll come right back. I even brought a good book to read." After we arrived, she gave me a kiss on the cheek and said, "Good luck! I love you."

"I love you, too," I replied. Walking back into the exam room, I already knew the drill. The nurse who was doing the PetScan said that he needed to take a blood test first to check my sugar levels. I did not remember having this done the first time, but I must have been so nervous that I forgot this part.

The nurse began by asking my birthday, then he said, "You're having this PetScan today because you had anal cancer."

Before I could answer him, I could tell by the look on his face that he knew I was ecstatic by his words, but he didn't know why. "I could hug you right now!" I exclaimed. "Yes, I *had* anal cancer. Thank you for using the word '"had'."

We both smiled, knowing how powerful that moment was between us. After he drew my blood and left, I sat in the recliner with a white blanket he had given to me to stay warm and to relax with. I could feel God's embrace through this white blanket. I was in tears when the man had used the word "had", and I had tears of joy again remembering this Godly moment. I knew as soon as the word came out of his mouth that this was a sign from God. God was speaking through him. I "had" anal cancer. I no longer have it. I was now excited to get my PetScan so that we could see this proof from God. Was I imagining this? There was no way that I was! This went through me and touched my Soul. I had a knowingness now. *Thank you, God, for this gift of awareness.*

An hour later, the nurse came back into the room to tell me it was time for my PetScan, and I realized time had gone by very fast; in fact, I had fallen asleep. This showed how relaxed I really was. I had no reason to be worried anymore.

He set me up on the PetScan table with my arms over my head and my white blanket covering me, then he left to start the scan. After only a few minutes he came back and asked, "Debra, do you have metal on your clothes?"

I said, "No, I don't. Is there something I forgot?" On your bra and on the front of your capri's," he explained.

My capri's had a draw string on the front, and where the string came out were two metal grommets. He told me my capri's would be fine. I could just pull them down to my knees, but that I needed to come down and get changed. If I felt comfortable wearing the shirt I had on without a bra, that would be fine, but if not he would bring me a gown. Thank goodness that my shirt was not tight; I was fine with my shirt.

Now, the nurse had to position my body again on the PetScan table. This time was interesting. He had two white blankets; One he placed on my body, then he had me put my arms up over my head. He placed the second white blanket over my arms, which was amazing because it felt like I had a halo over my head.

As the table began moving back and forth, I felt like I was surrounded by white light. The room was dark, but I could see this ray of light around my body. Was this God's white light shining through me? Was God working through this machine so that it would see His miracle?

I decided I would talk to God: *I can feel your warmth, comfort, light, and love. Thank you.* I wanted to embrace this magical moment. I would have never thought I would ever say getting a PetScan was a magical moment, but this was. I was breathing in this love that I was being surrounded in. I felt that the way the nurse put the blanket on was another sign to represent an angel was with me.

In that moment, I thought I felt someone touch my right arm and my left arm. Who were these Spirits that had come to embrace me and stand on both sides of my body above head? Being a medium, I asked: *who is here with me?*

I heard, *Debra, it's us; your mom and dad.*

Wow! Talk about powerful! They were with me during this scan. They didn't say anymore; in fact, I didn't feel them anymore, but I trusted that they were still with me, holding my arms to let me know we had this. I was not doing this alone.

My nurse came in to say the scan was done. As he turned on the lights, I raised my arms in the air, made a fist with my right hand, and swiveled my wrist around as I was coming out of the scanner for the last time. In my mind, I said, *Woohoo! Lesson done! Thank you, God!*

Getting off the table, I asked if he could make me a copy of these scans.

"Sure," he replied, "but you will have to go back into the room with the recliner and wait another half hour, as it takes some time. Unfortunately, you can't sit in the waiting room after having the radio-active drug put in your body."

I felt bad making Patty wait an extra twenty minutes, but I knew it was important, as this could be God's proof in these scans.

The twenty minutes went by fast. I had the CDs of the scans in my purse, and I felt like I had a skip in my step as I went to greet Patty. She was waiting with a smile on her face. She was so happy to see that I also had a smile and was okay. On the way home, she told me she went to have her coffee on the patio outside and then when she returned she read her book, so her time went by fast, too. We both decided we deserved to have a nice lunch out.

Returning home, I was tired, which most likely came from all the drugs they put in my body. I drank as much water as I could so that I could get them to go through me fast. I needed to call Cindy, Amy, Jan, and Valerie as I told them that I would. When I got Valerie on the phone, she said, "Debra, I need to share something with you. Today

I sat down in mediation at the same time that you were getting your PetScan. As I was praying for you, I saw your parents. They were quiet and calm. I saw them place their hands on your shoulders, one on each side."

I felt my grip tighten on my phone and my jaw dropped slightly. "Oh my goodness," I breathed. "Really? Valerie, you saw exactly what I felt! I felt two Spirits touching my arms that were above my head, and when I asked who they were, they told me they were my parents. And you're right; they were calm and quiet. You just validated to me that this was really them! Can you believe this? This is awesome! Spirit is awesome! My parents are awesome! This just made my day. Thank you."

I didn't even think of sharing this experience with the other three. Valerie was the last one I called. I did tell them about how my nurse had said, "Debra, you *had* anal cancer." My conversations were short with each of my friends because I knew I had to call everyone, plus it was close to dinner time and I didn't want to take them away from their families.

Going to bed that night, I had a lot to be grateful for. I knew I would fall asleep fast, so before I laid my head on my pillow I sat in prayer, thanking God for this amazing day and for the sign he gave of my parents being at my side and that I was not alone. He was right there at my side, shining His white light around and through me.

When I got the call with my scan's results, I was in the restroom and heard my phone ring out in the living room. By the time I got to it, the person had already left a message. I checked my voice message and it was Dr. Steven calling. I also noticed that the time of the call was 2:22. Had he not left the message, I would not have recognized the time.

My heart sank into my stomach when I realized I would be listening to his message by myself. Everytime I had to see my doctors to get results or talk to them about upcoming procedures, Amy was at my side. Now, I was alone. I took a deep breath and said, "God, please be with me. Hold me up and give me the strength to listen to this message." Then I pushed the arrow and listened.

"Hi Deb," spoke my doctor's kind voice that I knew very well by now. "It's Dr. Steven. I just want to let you know that your PetScan looks great. We don't see any sign of cancer at all in the scan. So, that is exactly what we were hoping for. Oh, I am seeing you on Wednesday, so I will show you in person then. I just wanted to give you the good news. Talk to you soon. Bye bye."

My breath was caught suspended in my throat the entire time I listened to his message. When I exhaled, I let out a cry. Tears flowed in relief, and I wanted to shout to the world: "I beat this beast! I no longer have cancer!"

I was in a state of perfect happiness. God's words "all is well and will be well" were exactly the way I had thought them to mean. I had to call Dr. Steven back, and he answered on the first ring.

"Dr. Steven," I began, "I just listened to your message. I am so grateful for everything that you and your team have done for me. The protocol that you designed for me was exactly what I needed. I can't thank you enough!"

"Debra," he replied, "we would do anything for you."

His words brought fresh tears to my eyes, and I could hardly get out the words, "Thank you, doctor. Have a wonderful rest of your day."

When we ended the call, I felt like jumping up and down with joy. I put my arms up in the air, shouting out loud in my house: "We did it! We did it! God, we did it!"

Now I needed to call my family and friends. I could only hope everyone would answer right away! I was so excited to share this miraculous news. Allison came walking in the door, home from school, and I shared the news with her first. "I am so happy for you, Mom!" she exclaimed and gave me a hug as I cried. "I knew you would be fine."

I called my children first. Stephanie she cried over the phone, saying, "I am so happy for you and with this news, Mom." I could feel the relief in her voice that I was now going to be fine. Steven and his wife were ecstatic and shouted, "Woohoo!Now let's celebrate! You kicked cancer's butt!" Brad said, "This is great news, Mom. You did it!"

I spoke to Amy next, who was so thrilled for me when I shared the good news. We chatted about my upcoming follow up appointments, and how she was still planning on taking me there and being with me through the last steps. Next I chatted with Cindy, Jan, and then Valerie. By then, it was getting late, so I called my neighbor Larry over the phone to see if it was too late for me to walk down and share the news with him. He told me to come right down.

We stood in his kitchen, and Larry had a very concerned look on his face; he even looked pale. As soon as I said I was cancer free, he exhaled and put his arms around me. It felt like he was going to collapse in my arms.

"Oh my God!" he sighed. "This is good news!" Tears were flowing when he added, "Debra, you had me so scared! The last time you called asking if you could come down because you had something you needed to share with me, you told me you had cancer. I was so worried that you were going to share bad news. Before your call, the anticipation was killing me."

I hugged Larry again and said, "I am okay."

He said again, "Thank you, God."

I was back sitting by my kitchen counter not much later when Allison got home from work. She said she bought me blueberry cheesecake for us to celebrate together. I was so touched that she did this for me. She wanted to make the good news I received today a celebration for me.

As we were eating, she shared with me how frightened she was when she first found out. "It really turned my life upside down, Mom," she confessed. "A lot of nights I would lay in bed crying, and thinking, 'will my mom be around to see me get married?' 'Will she get to meet my children?'"

"Honey," I began quietly, "what's so interesting is that as you were lying in bed wondering about all these things, I was doing the exact same. We both were feeling the same pain. I'm sorry for any pain that I have caused you, and that I am so excited to put this behind us."

After we were finished, we hugged and headed to bed. When a loved one is diagnosed with cancer, each person is affected in their own way. I found it was amazing how Allison and I were going through the same emotions and thoughts. This showed me how connected we truly were with one another.

Before I went to bed, I looked up the meaning of 222, as that was the time I received my news from Dr. Steven in Doreen Virtue's Angel Numbers book. The meaning was: "Your deep conviction manifests miracles and wonderful opportunities. Keep the faith!" Wow! This said it all.

I sat in prayer for a long time that night. I had a lot to be grateful for. I gave all the glory for this miraculous news of me being cancer free to God. I was given proof that day of God's work.

He worked through the doctors, through my medicine, and through the machines. Everything went hand in hand. I was eternally grateful to God for healing me, and for the work that I did being His instrument in healing others. I shed a lot of tears. I was releasing all or any fear that I may have been holding until I received this news.

I also experienced tears of joy. I was crying about everything. It felt like everything at that moment of hearing those words from my doctor lifted off of me. I no longer was carrying any weight of all the unknowns. I could now walk forward, and in doing so I would walk with an attitude of gratitude knowing that all will be well and was well. Thank you, God!

18

RENEWED

As I took Layla for her early morning walk, my phone rang. I answered and heard Dr. Stephanie on the line.

"Good morning, Debra. I have the results from your PetScan and wanted to let you know that everything came back clear. You no longer have cancer."

I smiled. "I'm sorry if I don't sound excited," I replied, "but Dr. Steven called me yesterday and shared this wonderful news already."

"Of course he did," She said. "Well, I am looking forward to seeing you later this afternoon."

In the back of my mind, I wondered why she reacted with "of course he did". It seemed like they had something going on between them that I didn't know about. My doctors knew each other well, as they worked together with planning their patients' care.

Amy picked me up right on time for my first appointment with Dr. Stephanie. Walking from the parking lot to the building seemed so much easier than it had ever before. I wasn't walking in to anything that was unknown or unfamiliar. I didn't have to search for the courage inside me to help me do this and or to give me strength when I was once so weak.

Today, my strides were confident and filled with strength and gratitude. This time walking in, I felt sad for everyone else that I saw who were struggling. As I walked past them, I said in my mind, *God, please surround them in your light and love like you did for me.*

The nurse took us both back to where she took my blood pressure. She made a comment that I must not have any worries or a care in the world today because I was 98/68. Amy and I both smiled at each other.

"No, I do not have any worries anymore," I replied. "I am cancer free."

Next I weighed in. I lost a total of seventeen pounds in six weeks. Now I understood why the doctors were telling me to bulk up. I lost so much weight and muscle mass in such a short amount of time. As the nurse walked us back to our room, she congratulated me for being cancer free.

Dr. Stephanie came in with a huge smile. I mentioned that it was interesting that we are all in the same room the first time we met. It felt like everything had gone full circle now, with me being in this room again but this time cancer free. I started to cry. It was such an emotional feeling.

I could remember my first day, and I was so grateful for this ending day. What was interesting to me was that we met every week for six weeks and never once was I placed in this same room. Dr. Stephanie and Amy both were astonished. This was amazing!

She told me that she would be my doctor for the next three years. They would follow up once a year with CT scans. Once I was clear for three years, I would be cancer free from this type of cancer for life; it will never come back.

I glanced at Amy and could tell that she wasn't happy with this news. She spoke up by raising her hand. "Why would you not do a scan sooner than a year? It seems that this would be too long of a time to wait in between, where something could come back. If we wait this long, we could be late at catching it once again."

"Amy," Dr. Stephanie replied, "we can't do CT scans that frequently on everyone. We would not have enough machines to do this with all the people we have to do scans for. Plus, insurance will fight us on this and most likely won't allow it. I feel confident that Debra will be fine waiting until next March to get her next scan."

We both trusted Dr. Stephanie, but also felt somewhat unsettled with her answer. I thanked her for all that she had done for me. The compassion she gave me meant a lot. I felt like I wasn't just another patient; I truly felt like she had my back.

She had to hand me a tissue, as I couldn't hold back my tears once again. During my care, we had made a special bond between us, one that I trusted and would continue to trust.

Afterward, Amy and I took the elevator down to the first floor and found Dr. Steven's office. This was our first time going to this particular office, and from the feel of it, I was glad that I had chosen to be seen at his other office. This one was newer, but the people at the desk were more business-like, where at the other office I was greeted every day by my first name. Maybe I felt this way because it was my first day.

Waiting in the room for Dr. Steven gave Amy and I more time to discuss the questions we should ask him. As usual, he walked in with a huge smile on his face.

"Hi ladies. We have some good news to go over. I have the before and after PetScans images of where your cancer was, Debra."

He pulled up the images of my first and most recent PetScans on his computer. Amy and I were both amazed with how much cancer was in my lymph nodes. The balls of cancer was huge in both of them, and the mass on the anal wall was big, too. This was another sign to me that God really did give me a miracle. Not one speck of cancer was left.

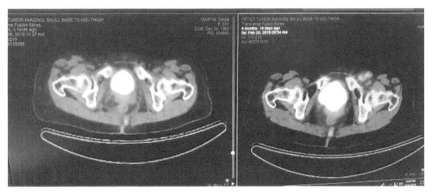

The Scan on 6/8/19 shows no cancer.   **The second scan on 2/20/19** shows cancer.

In the top right corner of the second image, there were two large round balls. These balls were the cancer that filled two of my lymph nodes on the left side of my body. In the first picture, I could no longer see the images of the balls in the lymph nodes. The center of the bottom of the second picture showed where the mass was on my anal wall. Dr. Steven had to point them out to us, as it was hard for us to see. The cancer was gone in both places! These images were taken four months and eighteen days apart.

It was fascinating for me to see what the before and after results looked like. I didn't realize how much cancer was actually in my body until then. I felt empowered by my results.

"Do you remember our first visit?" Amy asked Dr. Steven. "Do you remember what Debra told you?"

Dr. Steven nodded. "Yes, I do."

Amy said, "She told you she would be the one patient you had that her PetScans would come back revealing no cancer. At that time, you didn't want her to be discouraged if it showed some cancer on the first PetScan, because you said this was normal, as the cells were still dying and this could take time. Is what happened here rare?"

He just gave us a big smile and nodded his head yes. We didn't need any other explanation; we were good with his genuine way of answering.

I told Dr. Steven I had a gift for him.

"You probably want me to open this now in front of you, as it will most likely make me cry," he said. I told him he had to read the card before he looked into the bag. When he was finished reading, he said, "This is so cool. Thank you."

Inside the bag was a small blue flashlight, and when he turned it on its light shone bright. The words on the left side of the card said: "This flashlight is a symbol of your powerful presence when I found myself struggling in the dark. It's small and seemingly insignificant, but its powerful light will make a difference, just as you did for me."

I continued to say, "You really made me feel like I mattered. When I walked into the room having a bad day, you always had this big smile and changed my attitude by saying, 'Debra, you are doing great.' I always left feeling better than when I arrived. Thank you for being so caring and compassionate. These actions helped me in my healing process. I can't thank you enough."

"Okay," Dr. Steven said, "now you are going to make me cry."

We all stood up and he gave me a hug. "Have a great time with your family celebrating you," he said before Amy and I left.

Walking out of the cancer treatment center that day, I felt renewed. I could tell Amy felt good, too, as she said, "You did it! You beat cancer! You're all done! Yeah!" We hugged one another before we got into the car to head home.

"We did it!" I agreed. "Thank you!"

Before we went into the doctor's office, I gave Amy a flashlight with the same meaning. I planned on giving each person that helped me one, including my family, as they each helped me keep my light shining when I felt so grim. They gave me hope when I was losing hope. They each played a major role in my healing. Every time they would reach for that flashlight, they would remember me and what we went through together to get to this beautiful ending.

The next time I walked into this center again would be to get the results from my CT scans. I was not worried about these upcoming tests. God showed me and told me that all was well. He also said, "all will be well" and I trusted His words. These CT scans would continue to prove God's miracles of no cancer in me.

I had ten more days to get my strength up before leaving for vacation. I knew I needed to continue to honor my body and take the time to heal, but when I got one good day of feeling almost back to normal, I began to get anxious as I wanted my life back. I was feeling like I was done with all of this. I no longer had cancer, so why couldn't I go back to living my normal life right away? Instead of getting frustrated, I was grateful that I was able to exercise again, taking my time walking Layla, using my treadmill, light weights, and slowly beginning to do yoga again. I knew it was important to be patient with myself, and that getting back in shape would take time, but eventually I would accomplish this goal as well.

19

A CELEBRATION TO REMEMBER

I was up early the morning of July 20th because I was thrilled to be flying to visit my family. I was looking forward to seeing my driver JT again, as the last time I saw him was February 14th. He drove me to the airport after I met with my chemo and radiation doctors for the first time. This time, I would be able to tell him I am cancer free.

JT greeted me with a smile and loaded my suitcase in the trunk while Layla and I climbed into the back seat. He was so happy to hear my news. We had a lot to catch up with since we last saw one another. While I was sick, he had sent me a text to watch a Netflix movie that he and his wife enjoyed.

I told him I became addicted and couldn't stop watching the episodes. I was sad when it was over. We discussed how we both hoped Netflix will produce more sessions. Before long, we arrived at the airport. I thanked him for being so accommodating with all of my family. Everyone in my family enjoyed their rides with him to and from the airport. He said, "you're welcome, Debra. Enjoy your family vacation and see you when you return."

Walking through the airport had a totally different feeling than the last time. I was so grateful for being able to fly and for being healthy.

I had come along way; just a few months ago I would not have been able to make this trip or even walk in the airport. Today I carried Layla in her carrier plus an oversized shoulder bag. Everyone seemed so kind, more than I ever noticed before. Maybe they were feeling my attitude of gratitude and responding kindly back. Either way, I was feeling amazing.

When I arrived, Steven greeted me with a big hug. It was only a few months since he left my house when I had my last hug. This time was different; we both embraced, feeling happy knowing that I was cancer free. It wasn't like the last time when we were in the unknown phase, not knowing if I would even be able to make it to his house again. It felt so good to be there.

I was excited to see my daughter-in-law and grandkids. The last time I saw my grandson was a month after he was born, and now he was already nine months. He was growing up so fast! The weather in Ohio was extremely humid for the first two days, but it didn't bother me. I hung out with the kids and enjoyed my playtime with them inside.

They had a two story house and the air conditioning was working hard, but it wasn't cooling down the upstairs bedrooms, where the guest room and kids' rooms were. My granddaughter, who was four, and I decided it would be fun if we had a sleepover in the basement. Just she and I. Their basement was totally furnished and beautiful. We turned on one of her favorite stations and snuggled under several blankets as the basement was where the air conditioner was, so the room was freezing cold. I even put socks on to stay warm!

I cherished this special time with her. We always had a special bond between us; whenever I came to visit, she slept with me. The next morning, she put her head on my chest, looked up at me with her gorgeous eyes, and said, "I love snuggling with you, Dee Dee. I love you." This melted my heart. She could have been working me to turn on a movie and hang out with her longer rather than going upstairs and joining the rest of the family. She won me over. I was going to soak up this up as long as I could.

The next nine days were filled with exactly what my heart and soul needed to celebrate my victory. We took walks with Steven's family dog, Millie, and I was pleasantly surprised with my endurance. At the pool, my granddaughter and I had fun renting paddle boards and exploring the water that was designed to look like a beach. We had BBQs at night, and despite how happy I was, I became exhausted very quickly. This was more activity in one amount of time than I'd done in a while.

One night, I gathered my family together before some of Steven's friends would arrive. We all sat around the patio table outside. I shared from my heart how grateful I was to each of them for helping me during this hard time in my life. I became very emotional and could hardly speak. I handed them each a card where I wrote words just for them, along small bags that held flashlights. Their cards included the saying about the flashlight.

"This is just a small token," I said to them, "as there are not enough words or anything that I could buy that would say thank you for all you've done for me. I love you all."

It was my last night before going home, and I felt like crying. I had an overwhelming feeling that I was over-doing myself. The first five days were great, but then I started to feel more tired throughout each day; my body wasn't used to so much physical activity. I rested when I could, but it wasn't the same rest that I would get at home.

When I returned home, I was exhausted from my ten days of adventure and bliss with my family and their friends. I remembered my doctor told me to stay for only five days, and I knew I should have listened. He knew what was best for me, as he saw how people healed in this process with the type of cancer I had.

As the weeks went by, I witnessed that if I pushed myself I would pay for it later. One hour I felt normal, and then I was back to the way I was: the healthy me. I learned it was important that we give ourselves time to heal. I wanted to heal more quickly, but my body was saying, "not yet, sweetheart." It needed more time to build and repair. It went through a lot; my treatments were harsh. What others saw on the outside was nothing compared to the damage on the inside. Makeup couldn't cover up the damage on the inside. We need to treasure and cherish our vessel of our body by giving ourselves time to heal completely before taking on our previous lifestyles again.

My treatments were asking for respect and deserved this time. They did their part, and now I had to do my part to heal. We were in partnership, allowing the treatment to do what it was meant to do. This all went hand in hand. As a healer, this was what I always taught everyone, and now I was living it. I had to do my part in my own healing. I had always told my clients to not stop treatments when they were doing a healing session; they went hand in a hand, and I learned this firsthand.

As I glanced out my front windows one morning, I realized it was time for my roses to be trimmed. What were the odds of them needing this done exactly at the time that I was now able to trim them again? I gathered my gardening tools and Layla joined me happily in the yard. Trimming each bush stem by stem brought me so much joy.

I was feeling incredibly grateful; I was beginning to live my life again. I was taking one day at a time, and each step with gratitude for whatever was going to come my way. I learned not to sweat the small stuff and not to worry. That was a waste of my energy and time. I learned how to let go and let God. When I did this, it was eye opening how God would hold these worries and how free I would feel. This gave me the courage to walk through these difficult times, and it also helped bring balance to my life.

When I first learned I had cancer, I was very careful not to tell everyone. Some questioned me, wanting to know why I wouldn't want to share with everyone so they could pray for me. As a healer, I strongly believed in the power of prayer, but I also believed that when others spoke negatively about someone, that also went out into the universe.

What I meant by this was that if a lot of people were praying for me, that would also mean a lot of people were most likely saying things like: "Did you hear about Debra having cancer?" "I feel so sorry that Debra has cancer! Poor Debra." When someone says "poor Debra", it feels as though they are saying I lack, and I am without.

The truth was I really always had what I needed and more. How often do we say, "poor so and so"? Are we saying they do not have the inner gifts we all have, just because they are ill? We can show our compassion and still believe and trust in the Spirit within the person that is suffering.

I never owned having cancer. I said, "God, what is my lesson that you want me to learn from this?" See the difference? Had I owned it and shared it with others, I would now be hearing, "Debra, how is *your* cancer? How are you doing with Your Cancer? Are you still having symptoms from *Your* Cancer?"

At the end of my treatments, I said goodbye to cancer. I declared, "I will continue to live a life from here on without you. I no longer need you. I received what I needed from you."

I see every challenge as an opportunity. I didn't look at this as suffering or illness. If I did, then I would have stopped right there. Instead, I stayed open by asking the right questions: Why did I receive this? I am a healer. I do not understand. How could this have happened to me? Haven't I gone through enough? I have compassion for my clients. How could I need more as a healer? By asking these questions, I continued to grow and learn the lessons offered to me.

There were times that I started to become depressed. When this happened, I took a deep breath and said, "This is only happening now." I didn't want to give it anymore power. I perceived this as temporary and I would get through it. By telling myself this over and over, it allowed my brain to recognize and accept this. The words also gave me peace and a knowingness within that all would be well and is well. This was all part of my healing process.

You heard me refer to my cancer as the "beast" inside me. That was the case until I understood the cancer. The insight wasn't there in the beginning, because I saw it as an enemy that was destroying me. As I began to ask questions like "What do you have for me?", I learned from it. I saw its beauty. It was no longer the enemy. I understood what it gave me and why it appeared. I was able to then walk away from it. It was no longer a part of me. I now refer to it as the "Beauty and the Beast". I recognized the beauty that came from this beast.

I talked about my Army that I built around me. My Army was my team that was there to support me in every part of my healing process. I no longer looked at cancer as an enemy to be beaten, but as a teacher, and I was the student. I embraced the learning ahead. When one stops resisting the illness and instead seeks understanding, fear disappears, and in its place we discover the hidden blessings of growth and a new way of seeing.

I received an education through the experience I received. I am a better healer, as I am now on the same side as my clients, where before I was on the opposite side looking in. I didn't truly understand what they were going through until now. I had compassion, but not at the level that I do now.

This has given me more empathy for what others are going through, where I can now use my experience to help guide them in their own healing. I was witnessing this knowledge coming through me as I was healing others. I had accepted cancer as my teacher, and now I was becoming the teacher. I was using the tools that I was given through this experience in my healing sessions.

As a healer, I questioned if I should get treatment. I went into prayer. I had to trust my inner gut. When faced with this as a healer, I didn't know what to do. Was it okay to be a healer and seek medical advice? Some people thought it had to be one or the other, medicine or faith, but we are both human and soul, therefore we need both. It is a partnership. They work together, just like our soul and human body work together.

Through this journey with cancer, I now have a greater appreciation for my body, being human, and for life itself. I see the beauty surrounding me in every breath I take, every walk I take, and every moment that I get to live here on earth. When I am having a bad day, I will look for the one piece of joy in that day. Then I am grateful and grounded in peace where I can continue to walk with an attitude of gratitude.

It's really up to you; be willing to be open and embrace not what is happening *to you* but rather what is being *offered* for you. This was the awareness that shifted me, and now, once again, I am a new person.

"A Perspective of Debra's Journey from the Outside"

Written by Valerie Kwietniak

Cancer is a word we all hope we'll never hear, but when I heard the word from Debra's mouth, it felt personal and just plain unbelievable.

Here is a woman who takes care of herself, *and* she's a Healer for Pete's sake! Strange how when life goes awry, we all fall back on that reward-based way of living. Like children, we think we've lived a good life, we have a relationship with God, and we help others; therefore, we get gold stars and a life free from the bad stuff, right? Wrong! Debra's journey with cancer really showed me how all, and I mean *all* the stuff in our life can be used as fertilizer for growth. There was something even more profound that made a deeper impression.

As Debra explained, during treatment she was still doing her healings. This, to me, was amazing I may have secretly thought in order for us to be used as a Divine instrument, we had to be at our best, physically, emotionally, and spiritually. When I saw Debra offering her chemo-radiated body as a healing vessel for someone else, I was astounded to say the least.

I wanted to honor Debra's way of being during this time by not sharing what she was going through with anyone unless she gave me permission. It was hard not to tell her clients, especially when I would read the feedback from her clients thanking Debra for what they experienced. I thought, *Wow, you don't know the half of it!*

What Spirit was doing through Debra's exhausted, chemo-brained, nauseous body was indeed miraculous. This has made such an impression on how I look at the power surrounding us and within us. We are not merely struggling human beings: we are amazing, powerful, miraculous vessels, and if we yield to that. . .ALL HEALING BREAKS LOOSE!

Turns out cancer was an opportunity disguised.

Behind the Scenes

I witnessed how God worked behind the scenes. It all started when I did a healing for Brenda Baker, whose story is in my book "Proof of Miracles". Brenda had a profound healing where God came to her and healed her from the inner pain she suffered during her life. This is the miracle Brenda received; it wasn't the miracle I had wished for. Brenda passed before I had the chance to meet her.

Only a few days later, Brenda reached out to me from Heaven. She asked me, *Debra, do you want to grow your business?* I replied yes.

Then you need to hire someone, Brenda replied. *If you want to grow your business, you need to step aside and get some help. You need someone to answer and reply to all of your emails and do your scheduling so that you can concentrate on doing your healings and readings. You can't control it all. It won't work this way. You need to get everything in place. Call my friend Lynette; she will know who to send you. She will become your friend.*

I replied, *Brenda, you were so lucky to have such a loving group of friends surround you and be with you when you passed. I saw the picture of the "holding hands" that everyone formed with yours. It was beautiful.*

Debra, she said, *my friends will become your friends.*

I sat for a moment and took this all in. All of her friends would become mine. How could that be? I could not see how this would ever happen.

A few days later, after I kept feeling the nudges from Brenda, I called Lynette. The conversation went something like this: "Lynette, Brenda has sent me to you. She told me if I want to expand my business that I need to hire someone to help me with my scheduling, and that you would know who that person is."

Lynette's unique, contagious laugh rang over the phone, and I knew as soon as I heard it that she understood what Brenda was saying. I wondered if Brenda had spoken to Lynette like she had with me.

Lynette said, "I sure do. She is an angel just like you. The two of you would be perfect together. Her name is Valerie. Would you like her number or would you like me to contact her for you?"

I decided to let Lynette contact Valerie, as I really wasn't sure if I was ready or not.

Of course I was dragging my feet. One morning I woke up to an email from Valerie. She was telling me she was reading my book "Soul to Soul" and liked my chapter about my dog, "Joey".

I said to myself, "Really, Brenda? You pushed her to contact me! Now I have no choice but to talk to her about working for me."

One year from Brenda's passing, Lynette was having a gathering with the same people who were with Brenda when she passed. They were gathering for a celebration of life for Brenda. Valerie was one of them; I didn't realize Valerie was one of the people with Brenda when she passed, and her hand was one of the hands surrounding Brenda in the picture I saw. When Valerie shared that she was coming to Phoenix for this gathering, I was so thrilled. I suggested that we try to get together.

Valerie had a dear friend who I had the pleasure of meeting through Lynette. I knew she was not doing well with her health, and I asked Valerie to see if she would be interested in a healing session. I didn't want to push this, but I wanted to gift this to her. Valerie said, "Debra, she is driving with me to Phoenix!"

"Oh my gosh!" I exclaimed, "do you think she would be open to having a private in-person healing at my house? Discuss this on your drive and see what she says. Let me know."

What I learned later was she had wanted to reach out to me for a healing, but was waiting for the right time. How divine was that? Instead of the distant healings I normally did, she would receive one in person. I suggested that any of the other women with her at the house for Brenda's celebration would be welcome to join her. They could all be part of this healing for her.

I didn't know what this meant or how this was going to transpire. I knew we had the healing scheduled on a Friday afternoon, and I wasn't sure who would show up. To my surprise, six women showed up who were very close friends of Brenda's. I was speechless.

I gathered them all together in my living room and shared the story of how Brenda told me to get everything in order. I told Brenda that she was so lucky to have such loving friends surrounding and supporting her. But what was so amazing was she said these friends would come to me, and here you all are! They had all traveled from different states to be here. Brenda had orchestrated this. Her friends were now in my house.

I could hardly get the words out. I was so emotional and filled with love. I shared one important detail that Brenda said one year ago: "Debra, you need to get everything in place." What I thought this meant was that I needed Valerie so that my business could grow. I didn't know was that I needed everything in place because I too was going to have cancer like Brenda did. Mine would be a different form, but it was cancer. Had I not paid attention and listened to Brenda to call Lynette, I would have not met Valerie.

If I had never met Valerie, I would have never hired her and my business would have fallen. Valerie kept my business running when I couldn't. She was my angel, just like Lynette said she would be. Brenda knew what was going to transpire and she worked behind the scenes to make sure I would be okay and that my business would survive. This was the gift Brenda gave me for the healing she received. She also gave me another gift that I would cherish for a lifetime: the gift of six other women that I now call my "Brenda Friends".

I had no idea all six of them were going to come! I thought maybe a total of three, depending on how many I could fit in my healing room. Valerie helped me set it all up. All seven of us joined together as one for a healing for their dear friend. We each took our spots, with some of us sitting in chairs and some of us lying down. We closed our eyes and I began speaking.

What we didn't know was that as she was being healed, we each were receiving a healing as well. We each felt the healing love and knew something powerful had taken place, but didn't really know the extent of the healings until later when we each experienced our individual results. I always say when one is healed, we are all healed, and that is what happened that day.

During the healing, we were all taken on a spiritual journey where we received healing, light, and the love of God. Then from the light came Brenda. She was here to greet us each one by one. She whispered a word in each of our ears that only we could hear. No one else in the group could hear but the one receiving the message. I thought we were finished until she came and walked towards me.

Oh my, I was the one giving the healing not receiving. She came up to me and thanked me for her healing. She embraced me with her love. We were meeting each other for the first time, Spirit to Spirit. I will never forget how profound and powerful this moment was for each of us.

Brenda called us the "Sacred Seven". This was what we now call our healing session. It was sacred, and there were seven of us, and we would always cherish this. When the session was over, we gathered in the kitchen and each shared the messages that came through, and which one was for whom. I was in awe! Everyone was touched with healing light and love.

Then the beautiful lady we were all there to heal gave me a gift. She said I gave her a gift today and she wanted to give me one. I said it was not necessary. She pulled out a beautiful silver heart necklace. She told me this was a piece of jewelry her husband had purchased for her years ago, and she wanted to give it to me. She also mentioned the words on the necklace: "Footprints In The Sand".

I had tears in my eyes. "You have no idea how this gift means so much to me," I told her. "This was my father's favorite poem, and he is now in Heaven." I had just finished my cancer treatments and re-ceiving this showed me that my father had been with me through my entire journey.

After they left, I sat in gratitude for the remainder of the night, thanking God for the healing, thanking Brenda for all of her work she did for me behind the scenes, and for bringing all of her friends to me. This was a sacred day.

Two days later, I heard these words: *Debra, in your last two near death experiences, you heard and saw God. The first car accident you felt me stand behind you and heard my voice say, "Are you ready?". You questioned later who that voice was, and the answer you heard was, "I am the only one who can decide if you stay on earth or if it's time for you to come home."* I knew it was God in that moment.

The second time when you were sick, you crossed over and wit-nessed me carrying you. You saw your body in my arms. Have you ever questioned where I have been while you were going through cancer?

I answered in my mind, *I felt you in my healing sessions. I felt you in my daily prayers and I never felt alone. I trusted you were with me each step of the way.*

Then I heard, *I was with you each step of the way. I was carrying you, just like the footprints in the sand.*

Oh my, now this was powerful and profound. I was sobbing. So when I said my father was carrying me, it wasn't my biological father; it was my Heavenly Father. *You have been orchestrating this all behind the scenes, every step of the way. You had a plan for me and gave me the gift of knowing that I will share with others who come to me for healing.*

I kept my faith every step of the way, and it was you that healed me with your healing light in my healing mediations. You healed me through the doctors as you gave them the wisdom they needed to heal me, and through the chemo medicine that you help make, and through the radiation machine that you sent your healing light through. Each went hand in hand. . .your healing hands, sending light and love through them all.

I thanked God for these guided prayers and for my doctors. He placed both of my doctors in my path, both of whom had my children's first names. That was my first sign! I felt this then and I know this now. God was my courage that carried me through these difficult moments. He was my strength. Thank you, God, for healing me of cancer. I have learned the lesson to share.

A Breakdown of the Tools and Lessons I Learned from Spirit and God

As you are facing the renewed YOU, place this fear into God's hands. When you do this, acknowledge any old feelings that may surface. Thank God for these, then say, "I no longer need these; they don't serve me. I am no longer going to hold onto them. I am shedding these so that I can be a new me, the masterpiece God created me to be." Then see yourself in your mind wearing a beautiful white gown, swirling around like a dance in God's white light. Celebrate this new you!

"Let Go and Let God" has really helped me in my healing journey. I know that everything is in Divine order. God is planning and putting things in order behind the scenes months and even years prior to us going through them. Letting go and letting God allows us to trust the process, knowing God has our back. We as humans have to feel to heal. This is what makes us who we are today. I placed everything in my prayers and watched it all unfold.

I walked through every door and then trusted my inner guidance. I saw the signs from Spirit with each step I took, giving me the validation that I was making the right decisions.

We feel to heal. Acknowledge what you're dealing with, release it, shed it, and rejoice. Sometimes you may cry, and tears are releasing this from you. The flood gates are open. Don't be afraid to cry. Embrace and know God will hold you through this process if you ask. Pray every step of the way.

Healing is a process. The doctors said it would be one year before I would have the same energy level that I had before I started my treatments. At first, I didn't believe this, but now I do. I will honor my body and allow these limitations, doing my part to heal. I would ask you to do the same when you are healing from any type of illness.

As I continued to heal others, I didn't lay down and say, "I can't to this sacred work that I was given." God showed me that my spirit was stronger than my body, and so is yours. Our Spirit can accomplish so much more if we trust and if we are open.

I trusted the doors that God opened for me. I always dressed for the occasion.

This cancer wasn't my downfall; it was me rising. It's how we choose to see it.

I kept a positive attitude, which helped me in my healing process. Try to stay focused on the now and try not to look ahead. It can seem daunting if you do.

Fear can get in the way of the spirit. Turn this fear into faith in knowing you can get through anything with God. God can make the impossible possible. Keep your light shining.

Cancer is hard for others to see. It's not like seeing someone with a broken bone. People will compare one cancer with another. Cancer is cancer! If you're receiving chemo or radiation, it is meant to kill the cancer, but it also destroyed everything in me. In doing so, it practically has to kill you.

Always voice your truth. I had to voice when I was tired or when something was too much. This wasn't easy! I am the type of person who can't sit around and look at the things that need to be done or help with things that need to be done. My brain won't allow it, so it pushes my body to do it. In the end, I became extremely exhausted. I am able to see this clearly now, as I come to the point of being so overwhelmed that I will start to cry for no apparent reason. Then I would get mad at myself for allowing myself to get to this point. Pay attention to your body and how it is reacting, and then honor it with love.

Having people around me the entire time of my treatments helped me stay focused. Without them, my mind would have had more time to wonder and worry. Depression would set in. You feel alone as you're going through an illness. It is frightening. It's important to allow people in during these difficult times, as isolating yourself just makes the pain worse. Everyone filled my home with laughter, comfort, and love.

When I was home alone, I was lonely. I learned that having each of my loved ones around me helped keep my mind positive and focused on other things rather than focusing on the bad or the pain that I was going through. This played a huge role in my healing process. This love and compassion brought me joy to each and every day, which helped heal me.

Humor is one of the tools that gets us through the tough times. Try to bring as much of this into each day.

Laughter is a key to healing.

Find a piece of joy in every day, even if it's a simple as you made it out of bed today, or you did one load of laundry, or that you were even able to talk on the phone. Let these simple acts bring you joy.

Make goals for yourself. This really helped me. I set goals each week that I could get through all of my treatments. I took it day by day, and at the end of each day I placed a star on my calendar as a reward to let myself know that I completed my goal. I also set a goal to finish my book "Proof of Miracles" and have it in print by March 21, 2019, and it was available the next day on Amazon. I started writing this book in May of 2019 and I had a goal to finish it by the end of August of 2019. I finished the draft to send to my editor on September 1, 2019. It's healthy to make goals. It gives you something to focus on and strive for. It gives you a purpose to keep going when you least feel like it. It's the goal that helps you move forward.

I was given a gift of time with each one of my children. Had I not had this cancer, we would not have had this quality alone time where we learned more about one another. Our love grew stronger.

When I questioned God, I didn't have the understanding and the compassion for people who were dealing with cancer or any other illness like I do now. I thought I did, but how could I really if I never experienced it myself? God was teaching me and showing me what others were going through. I now have more empathy than I have ever had before because I went through it. Through God's grace, I received more empathy than I had before. I now have a better understanding of what my clients go through with cancer. God knew what he was doing; he was making me a better healer.

Through my healing process, I removed all of my fear and embraced my doctors, my radiation machine, my chemo pills, and my treatments with love. We have to voice our concerns to our doctors and be an advocate for our bodies. Find the doctors you trust. If one doctor won't do what you feel is necessary, get a second or even third opinion. Doctors are practicing medicine; they are still learning with each patient they see.

It's okay to speak up. This can be hard, because we feel doctors are the specialists, and we think they know best. But they are human, too; they can't know everything for everybody. Since everyone is different, and each case is different, it's important to develop a trust and understanding with your doctor. I was able to develop a deep trust with both Dr. Steven and Dr. Stephanie. I still voiced my concerns for my body, and they helped guide me each step of the way. I helped them guide me by sharing with them my symptoms, concerns, and questions. I felt God chose them to play an important role in my healing process.

Sometimes you may feel familiar pain that you had felt prior to your treatments. This may cause you to think that it has come back. Many times these symptoms you are feeling are just part of your healing process. An example was when an itching would occur, which made me aware of my hemorrhoid. When itching came back again after my treatments, I was concerned that this was another hemorrhoid. I learned that I was itching from my radiation. This was part of my healing process. I had to feel to heal. Now I had to keep my faith and stand strong and say,

"I am healthy, I am whole, I am healed."

Every now and then our body may get unbalanced. This is spirit's way of reminding us to stay on the path to wellness, and stay on the path to maintenance. This is a reminder to get us back on track with our wellness. That's what we all learned from our illness; to take care of ourselves, to nurture ourselves, and to love ourselves.

Have the courage to walk through this and know you are never alone. Take one step at a time and try not to over think. When you do, pray. Ask for strength and comfort during each step. God will hold you and guide you.

I had a good outcome, but not everyone will have this same outcome. Some may be in hospice. Never give up hope. It's between you and God on when it's your time to go home.

I am not a fan of when the doctors give a diagnosis of how long someone has here on earth. There have been people in hospice that beat all odds. You will know when and if it's your time. At that time, embrace the love that surrounds you and know you are going to a place that is all about love.

Cultivate a life of gratitude so during those difficult times that is what is going to be with you.

Never lose hope.

Live life to the fullest.

ACKNOWLEDGEMENTS

I started writing this book before I received my results, not knowing what the ending would look like. I wondered what the results would be, but I trusted every step of the way.

I have so much gratitude to everyone who supported and loved me. You were all part of my Army that helped me heal. I am forever grateful to each and every one of you for the role you played in my healing journey.

I thank my family for all the sacrifices each of you made. You stopped your lives to help save mine, and you held my hand and walked beside me so that I never felt alone. You allowed me to speak my truth and be vulnerable. I may not have been the easiest patient to take care of, but through this we have lots of memories we can now laugh at. I thank each one of you for giving me unconditional love like I have never felt before. Love heals.

My friends, who checked on me and gave me support, love, and brought laughter into my life.

Valerie, who always gave me strength when I needed it. She was always saying I was doing so well. She saw what I didn't see. Thank you for the endless conversations we shared when writing this book. You helped me tweak my words so that they had more meaning and were more powerful. Valerie was my savior. Without her, I would have lost my business. She kept everything flowing.

Jan, for always being a phone call away and answering whenever I needed to talk. You always made me feel like you were right by my side, holding my hand each step of the way. Thank you for giving me hope when I was losing it. You always knew I would beat this beast!

Amy, I could not have done this without you. Without you, I would not have made it to every appointment. You were the one who kept everything organized. You were my voice to the doctors when I needed questions to be asked, and you physically held my hand each time I cried during my these appointments, or embraced me with a hug when I needed one. You gave me the courage to know I could do this. You would always say: "You got this, girl!" Thank you for being my rock!

Amy's Family, thank you for changing around your busy schedules so that it allowed Amy to be by my side each day.

Erin, for the calendar you made. It helped me set goals so I was able to see that I was accomplishing them day by day. Each star that I placed on the calendar showed me I was one day closer to Completion Day.

Patty, the angel next door who watched over me when others couldn't, and who would sit with me many nights until I fell asleep and be at my bedside when I woke up. Thank you for giving me the peace in knowing I could call you at all hours of the night. Before this happened, you always turned your phone off every night.

Larry, for the countless healthy meals you made at your house for me and my family so that I wouldn't smell the food. You always checked on me to make sure I was eating, and you always spent time hanging out with me. Thank you for all the joy you brought into my daily life.

Lynn, Jeff, and Pam, for taking the time to check in with me even when you were on vacation. You shared all your funny stories of what had transpired in your day and made me laugh. Thank you for always up-lifting my spirit and making me feel so loved.

Susannne Wilson, who nudged me to write this book. She recognized the potential that my words would have in helping others.

JT, for taking over all the airport pickups and dropoffs. You lifted a huge weight off my shoulders. I knew I could always count on you.

Doctor Steven and Doctor Stephanie, I feel such gratitude for the doctors that God placed in my path and who God used as His instruments in helping me heal. They both had such compassion and made me feel like I mattered.

Radiation nurses, Denise, Joni, and Brandi, thank you for greeting me everyday with a smile, caring for me, and for treating me not just like another patient. All of you got to know me as a person. With every treatment, you three helped me get through by making me feel like I could do this, and that you were proud of me for each step I accomplished.

Hannah, thank you for your editorial assistance and for helping me make this book come to life.

My faith has more depth, and my trust was built up through this journey. God showed me how He worked through me what was possible when I felt it was impossible.

God, thank you for carrying me through this journey and for these lessons. I give my word that I will use this knowledge to help others and to continue to walk in your light. The relationship I cultivated during my life led to to the partnership that gave me exactly what I needed to walk through this illness with courage, strength, and peace. I am eternally grateful for the lessons, tools, and healing gifted to me on my journey with cancer.

All of you became part of my Army. You each played a role in my healing process which I am forever grateful for. I will always carry in my heart the love that you gave me. I love you all, with all my heart.

Note from the Author

Thank you for reading this book. I hope this book gave you the knowledge to know that you are never alone, and that you have an inner connection with God. God is made of light and love, and so are we. Give yourself permission to take time to connect to your higher self and the essence of who you are through prayer and/or meditation habits. This will help you find joy and peace within. Lead your life with love and surround yourself with those you love.

May you be blessed with an abundance of good health in body, mind, and soul, and may you always have the awareness of God's love, light, and compassion.

Remember our greatest hardships bring us our greatest lessons, which brings us awareness. In this awareness we can see the blessings of what we have endured.

With faith, hope, gratitude, love, and peace,
Debra Martin

About The Author

Debra Martin is certified by the University of the VERITAS Research Program, which was co-directed by Dr. Julie Beischel and Dr. Gary Schwartz. She currently serves as a Certified Research Medium at the Windbridge Research Center where she participates in afterlife studies performed by Dr. Beischel. Debra has a natural ability to connect to spirits of those love who have passed on. She has helped countless people navigate the path of their grief and guide them through stages of healing.

Debra Martin is a world-renowned intuitive healer. After a lengthy illness as she was close to death on 01-21-12. Debra had an out of body experience which entailed seeing and conversing with God. She was given a choice to leave her family or go back to her earthly home.

Having made a commitment to God, she came back with a mission and a gift of healing. Debra is now a divine healing instrument and has shared her story on international radio shows. She has created a unique healing technique used nowhere else in the world, and witnessed miracles through God. She uses her gifts as a healer and as well as a medium to bring hope and healing, touching and changing people's lives worldwide.

She is an author of five books: "Believe Beyond Seeing", "Me and My Angels", "Soul to Soul", "Proof of Miracles" and is a co-author in the book "Direct Connect to God". All are available on Amazon.

Debra has been featured in national media, including A&E documentaries: Mediums: We See Dead People (2006) and Psychic Children and their Sixth Sense (2006), and has appeared in various news reports. One in particular, "The Medium Who Solved A Murder" gained international attention and was on the cover of the November 2015 Psychic News Magazine.

This was also broadcasted in 2007 by the Phoenix, Arizona CBS network affiliate and gained national attention. Debra has appeared twice on Coast to Coast AM with Georg Noory. Debra is featured in the documentary The One Who Comes After currently in production, which is produced and directed by Robert Narhotz.

Debra was ordained as a healing minister at The Logo's Center in Scottsdale, Arizona in November 2013.

Debra resides in Scottsdale, Arizona. When she is not working she enjoys traveling, hiking and relaxing by her pool with friends and family. She also enjoys what she calls her "God time", which is time spent in meditation and or prayer.

Visit Debra's Website at www.goldenmiracles.com and feel free to sign up to receive her newsletter. You can email Debra to request a healing or a reading at goldenmiracles@cox.net. Follow Debra on Facebook at www.facebook.com/debra.martin.3557, where you can read testimonials of her healings and readings.

To request a prayer for you or someone else, please go to Debra's Facebook Prayer page at www.facebook.com/DebraMartinsPrayerPage.

Debra created the Power of Prayer Facebook because she receives many requests for prayers. The intention for this prayer page is to help all those who are in need of emotional, physical, or spiritual healing. Her hope is to gather as many people throughout the world to join her in holding these scared requests in loving prayer.

Debra believes in the power of prayer. As we pray for one another, we raise our vibration that will travel like energy to those in need. Her intention is for everyone to be embraced with God's love and receive the miracle they deserve.

When one is healed, all are healed. Together we heal.

Debra highly recommends the Helping Parents Heal organization to anyone who has lost a child. Helping Parents Heal is a non-profit organization that helps parents transition from "Bereaved Parent" to "Shining Light Parent", through support and resources that aid in the healing process.

HPH goes a step beyond other groups by allowing the open discussion of spiritual experiences and evidence for the afterlife in a non-dogmatic way. Affiliate groups welcome everyone regardless of religious or non-religious background, and allow for open dialog. To learn more or to join Helping Parents Heal, please visit their website at www.helpingparentsheal.org

Debra has a great passion for the Andy Hull's Sunshine Foundation. Feeling that death by suicide is far too common, LeAnn Hull turned her pain into power and created Andy Hull's Sunshine Foundation. The focus and mission of the foundation is to provide awareness and prevention of suicide with a "You Matter" approach. To learn more about this Foundation please visit https://andyssunshine.com/

Becoming a certified research medium and being studied by scientists provided me with evidence that what I was receiving was real and the confidence to use my mediumship to help others. I would not be who I am today without that history. Science has been and continues to be my backbone.

Most scientific fields are funded by government agencies but there is no funding like this for mediumship and life after death studies. Please donate to the Windbridge Research Center so that we all can continue to grow and learn more about the afterlife through their research. To donate, go to www.windbridge.org/donate

Made in United States
Troutdale, OR
11/29/2023